BEATLE WIVES

THE WOMEN
THE MEN WE LOVED
FELL IN LOVE WITH

NY Times Best-seller
MARC SHAPIRO

For more information contact:
Riverdale Avenue Books
5676 Riverdale Avenue
Riverdale, NY 10471

www.riverdaleavebooks.com

Design by www.formatting4U.com
Cover by Scott Carpenter

Digital ISBN: 9781626015999
Paperback ISBN: 9781626016019
Hardcover ISBN: 9781626015999

First Edition: November 2021

This Book is Dedicated to:

All the women in my life who have never been a Beatle Wife.

The love of my life Nancy. Still my everything after all these years.

My daughter Rachael who continues to carry her personal and professional life with style, grace and enthusiasm.

My agent Lori Perkins who has always been the hardest working, most honest, no BS person in the literary world.

Finally, to all the wives, daughters, significant others and women of all orientation and persuasion… I salute you.

Table of Contents

Author's Notes
Not Just Another Beatle Book

There have been literally hundreds of books about The Beatles over the years.

The history of the Fab Four as a legendary band has been told countless times, as have detailed biographies of John, Paul, George and Ringo. Important pivotal moments in the band's career have been reported at length in books several hundred pages long. Discographies. Filmographies. Quote books. Trivia books. Photo books both formal and informal. The fascination with The Beatles continues unabated. The more you give Beatle fanatics, the more they want to know.

I wrote a Beatle book some years ago entitled *Behind Sad Eyes: The Life of George Harrison*. It was an honest, no punches pulled look at the 'Quiet Beatle' and it did quite well. As has literally every Beatle book ever written.

But even the best, most researched and most often cited books have had their flaws. With many, there was an agenda to propagate, an element deemed not quite as important to the story as others. Occasionally, there would be a sense of incomplete to many of them. In many of them, it always seemed that something was missing.

For instance… Even the most successful of these tomes has, with rare exception, given the wives of the Beatles historical short shrift. Most often, the wife of a Beatle has been condensed into a cipher, someone with little substance or consideration other than being the 'wife.' When wives have been showcased at all, it has most often been as a mirror to the flawed nature of the husbands, watching as affairs, drug taking, etc., piled up around them and, occasionally, to mirror the wives' own indiscretions in the face of their spouses' bad behavior and often overwhelming fame.

And when, historically, things in the lives of The Beatles went critically or personally wrong or ventured into petty gossip, the hatchet of public opinion has often fallen on the necks of Beatle wives, leaving bloody marks.

To this day, Yoko Ono is still considered by many as the person who, single handedly, broke up The Beatles even though the band was well on the way to breaking up before she entered the picture. And who comes out smelling like a rose in the George Harrison/Eric Clapton bromance? Certainly not Patti Boyd who, according to several books, had her own moral lapses while married to George. Even the largesse of Paul McCartney in letting his wife Linda sing live on stage and occasionally in the studio turned on her rather than him when it was discovered and propagated over the years that Linda was often embarrassingly off key.

But it was to their collective credit that none of the Beatle wives ever totally ran for cover.

During the heyday of Beatlemania and beyond, most were accessible to the press and, when asked, were not shy about sharing their feelings about the care and feeding of a Beatle husband. But there was that frustration that had to be brewing when their personal lives became completely overshadowed with questions that began and ended with variations on the theme of 'What was it like to be the wife of a Beatle?'

Pure and simple, the wives of The Beatles have never been given center stage, let alone a legitimate day in the sun. Until now.

The idea behind *Beatle Wives: The Women the Men We Loved Fell in Love With* was centered around the notion of turning the tables, making these women the center of attention on all fronts and moving their famous husbands to the background, appearing largely in shadow and then only as their actions and anecdotes pertain to their wives. In conception, the idea of a book focusing on the wives was a bit of a gamble. How interesting would a book on The Beatles that did not feature The Beatles in a featured role go down? But these are different times and the angle this book would take seemed worth the risk.

From the beginning, the idea was to document the nine Beatle Wives in extensive detail, literally from birth to death and/or the later stages of their lives. Who and what they were before meeting their famous husbands, the courtships from their point of view, how they became part of the Beatle universe and, most importantly, how they moved, personally and creatively within it. There would be a new take on it all, a feminist/modernist look at these women, philosophically and socially, abroad in a strange new universe. We would see the humanity, the faces and the personal and professional challenges they faced, all wrapped up in a bit of history whose relevancy is valid well into the 21st century.

Early love and marriage for individual Beatles came at a turbulent time. There were changes socially, politically and sexually at every turn. Beatlemania was raging around the world. Everyone wanted to know The Beatles and, by association, everyone wanted to know who these young superstars fell in love with and married. And years later, with equal rights on so many levels a serious issue, the modern world looks back at the women who married The Beatles and still wants to know who they are.

And in the tradition of six degrees of separation, I had my own real-life encounter with a Beatle wife to throw into the mix.

Back in 1974 when I was one of countless, faceless freelance journalists in Hollywood trying to turn a buck, I landed a gig writing press bios for a start up record label called *Dark Horse Records*. The significance was not lost on me. *Dark Horse Records* was founded and operated by George Harrison. During several visits to the Dark Horse offices, I dealt with an office assistant named Olivia Arias. The shorthand impression was that Olivia was kind, professional and to the point. Yes it was that Olivia who would go on to marry George Harrison.

As with all Beatle ventures, *Beatle Wives: The Women the Men We Loved Fell in Love With* lived and died by an extensive amount of research. And along the way, there were many surprises. Through the eyes of these women, I found the strength in these women as well as the heretofore emotional frailty of their famous husbands.

In a sense, writing this book was relatively easy. The nuts and bolts of The Beatles and their lives have long been set in stone. The names and dates have not been changed to protect the innocent. But the difficult part, and perhaps the most important part, was stitching together pivotal moments from the wives' perspective.

But anyone who thinks research on a project so expansive was easy, guess again. Reality reared its ugly head. A lot of interview requests were met with the sound of crickets. For better or worse The Beatles have been done to death and those with any kinds of stories to tell were not interested anymore. Fortunately in most cases there was a mountain of paperwork to discover and to consider. This was the hard work, mixing and matching attitudes and anecdotes, correcting misconceptions and knowing how and in what manner to put the often-neglected wives in the driver's seat. And along the way a new attitude emerged.

There was a lot to consider.

But there was also a lot that was new and the discoveries were seemingly around every corner. What many short-sighted observers tend to forget was that many of these women had quite substantial careers before they married a Beatle, careers that, for the most part, they continued to carry on during their marriages. These are women of some intellect, creativity and the strength to be, by degrees, largely independent and down to earth in the face of the Beatle insanity that was swirling around them. And let's not forget that although their husbands were driven when it came to their music, they would often turn to their wives, or be not too subtly, influenced by them in their everyday lives. In many ways, the Beatle wives were a legitimate driving force in the lives of their men and what the experience made for themselves.

The lives of the wives of The Beatles are not simply a matter of luck, timing and, at least on the surface, a fairy tale come true. Being the spouse of any celebrity has never been easy. Being the wife of a Beatle could be particularly daunting. Watching and living in the vortex of a worldwide cultural explosion was seemingly insurmountable. That was the reality of it all, the ups and downs and hows would ultimately change the women forever.

This was a project that had a profound impact. My perspective was turned around and resulted in attitudes changed. I got a lot out of this. It was not just another Beatle book. It was a journey into a whole new way of thinking.

Marc Shapiro 2021

Introduction
Before There Were Wives

They were young, brash, creatively driven, funny, attentive, occasionally controlling and manipulative and, yes, even a bit dangerous. There was a lot in the psychological and emotional makeup of John, Paul, George and Ringo that had always made The Beatles attractive to women and young girls.

And, in later years, the women who would become their wives would often recall those first magic moments.

Upon the occasion of meeting her future husband, John Lennon, for the first time, Cynthia Lennon told *Classicbands.com* that "It was just an instant attraction. It was probably from the inside, not the outside. There was something about him that was for me. I wanted to know who he was and what he was."

Yoko Ono, in the book *John Lennon: The Life* was equally enthralled. "We were both so excited about discovering each other. We didn't stop to think about anybody else's feelings. We just went ahead gung ho."

For her part, Patti Boyd was breathless in her autobiography *Wonderful Tonight* about the day she first laid eyes on George Harrison. "George with his velvet brown eyes and dark chestnut hair was the best looking man I had ever seen. Being close to him was electrifying."

Women being enraptured by The Beatles is not a phenomena that began with the women who married them. By the time John, Paul, George and Ringo were entering their teen years and years before even The Quarrymen had formed, young women were meeting, romancing and forming their own opinions about the future Fab Four.

When Barbara Baker and Lennon were younger, he would often harass her with taunts of 'horse face.' But by the time both were in their teens, attitudes changed. According to such diverse sources as *TodayI FoundOut.com*, *John Paul & Me Before The Beatles* by Len Garry and

1

Sentstarr.com, Lennon had turned into a typical 16-year-old teenage horn dog who had only one thing on his mind. Baker, who had evolved into quite the beauty, was that thing. Lennon would show his good side, asking her out for walks in the park and bike rides. But it would not be long before the lecherous Lennon took over. Baker's earliest reflections of Lennon was that he had "charm" and that "he was good with the ladies back then."

It would not be long that they were going steady. Not only would their relationship be Lennon's first serious dalliance but it would also result in the first time he had sex. As the relationship progressed, Baker would see both sides of her lover. Lennon could be very courteous and, as she offered in *TodayIFoundOut.com*, downright romantic. "He was a very romantic boy, extremely romantic. He wrote pages and pages of poetry to me."

But as Baker would discover that Lennon was just as likely to be cruel and disrespectful. Almost immediately after losing his virginity, Lennon took the news to all his friends, describing the incident with totally unflattering terms directed at Baker. And she would later discover, as reported in the book *John, Paul & Me Before The Beatles*, that just about everything they did sexually was getting back to his chums. "I remember a night or should I say a day in my teens when I was fucking my girlfriend on a gravestone and my ass got covered in greenfly," it was reported in the book.

Baker and Lennon would be on and off for a reported two years before splitting for good. Not surprisingly, Lennon would move onto other women with his largely chauvinist/sexist attitude intact, according to another girlfriend Thelma Pickles in *Beatlesarama.com*. "He certainly didn't have a romantic attitude to sex. He had a very disparaging attitude to girls who wanted to be involved with him but wouldn't have sex with him. He was no different than any young bloke. If he felt you were leading him on but would not have sex with him, he'd be very abusive. With John it was entirely about lust."

Dorothy 'Dot' Rhone was a shy, awkward 16 year-old in 1959 when she did something quite out of character. She attended a gig at the notoriously decadent Casbah Club where an up and coming band called The Quarrymen was performing. At one point in the evening, she struck up a conversation with band members John Lennon and Paul McCartney. She initially fancied Lennon but when she found out that he was already involved, she set her sights on McCartney as she offered in *TodayIFound Out.com* and *Senstarr.com*.

"Paul was handsome in a softer way than John. I liked that. So we

2

"My first shag was in Hamburg with John, Paul and Pete (original drummer Pete Best) watching," Harrison recalled in the book *Behind Sad Eyes: The Life of George Harrison.* "We were in bunk beds and they really couldn't see anything because I was under the covers. But after I finished, they applauded and cheered. At least they kept quiet while I was doing it."

Geraldine McGovern and Ringo Starr had been neighbors for some time before they began dating in 1957. Consequently McGovern knew exactly who Starr was. "Richie was shy in a way," she stated in *Sentstarr. tripod.com* article culled from several interviews she did in the 60's. "He was determined to be famous but he wasn't at all flamboyant about it."

Starr was like many young men of the day, aspiring to fame and fortune while always being pressured be family to get a safe, stable job. But there was a lot about the couple that made them imminently compatible in a relationship that would last four years. McGovern would be patient in the relationship that saw Starr's passion for music come first. "His music always came first," she recalled in *Sentstarr.* "He was playing most nights and if I wanted to see him, I had to go along with him. We were never able to have much time together."

Still, the relationship flourished and after three years, the couple were preparing for marriage. There was an engagement ring and a tentative date. "I was engaged and I did love her and she loved," Starr said in *Sentstarr.* "We made all the preparations to go into marriage."

But the fly in the ointment still remained Starr's passion for music. He was in an up and coming band called Rory Storm and The Hurricanes but McGovern was pressuring him, in light of the marriage plans, to give up his passion in favor of a stable job. Adding to the pressure was the news that Rory Storm and The Hurricanes landed a prestigious and lucrative residency at a summer camp. McGovern painfully recalled in *Sentstarr* how the news essentially put an end to their relationship.

"That really ruined the relationship when he went off to that job, I told him I didn't want him to go. We talked it over. There was no shouting or slagging. But that was the end."

By the early 60's, what had been The Quarrymen had evolved into The Beatles. The consensus was that The Beatles were about to break very big. But as their earliest relationships with women had proven the members of the band were still essentially children when it came to dealing with women as grown up men. With the success, there was a new wave of women who were about to enter their lives. Women who would love them, test them and prove, in their own ways, that they could drive them and influence them and still remain true to themselves.

Chapter One
Cynthia Lennon

Cynthia Lennon was a chameleon. Not so much in the way she presented herself to the world as it was as the world perceived her. One thing was certain and that was that Cynthia had a keen perception of how people looked at her.

"I was usually dismissed as the impressionable young girl who fell for him [John Lennon] and then trapped him into marriage," she related in her book *John*.

Hunter Davies, the notable author and Beatle chronicler, was succinct regarding Lennon in a conversation with the *BBC*. "She was not a hippie at all. She was seen [by many] as refined and reserved."

Steven Gaines, the co-author with Peter Brown of the controversial Beatles' tome *The Love You Make* waxed somewhat poetic in a *Vulture.com* piece in describing Lennon. "Cynthia was a lovely person, sweet, soft spoken and shy. She was also a melancholic figure, wistful, smoking cigarettes and drinking white wine into the small hours."

She was born into a middle class British family. By all accounts Charles Powell and his wife Lillian were living the idyllic existence. Charles made a comfortable living selling General Electric electrical goods to all the shops in Liverpool while Lillian, a stay-at-home wife and mother to their two sons Charles and Anthony, was beaming with the news that the couple was about to bring a third child into the world. But all that changed in 1939 when World War II was declared. Fearing impending attacks from the Germans, the decision was made that Lillian would relocate, for safety's sake, to a tiny bed and breakfast in the seaside town of Blackpool. Lillian went into labor on September 9 and endured labor for a day and a half until a midwife could be summoned to assist in the birth.

Cynthia Powell was born on September 10, 1939.

After Cynthia's birth, the Powell family was reunited and relocated to a two-bedroom house in the town of Holylake, just across the river from Liverpool. Cynthia grew up a quiet and, by degrees shy child, who early on showed a talent for drawing and art which her parents readily encouraged. During what would be her final interview with *Living on Mallorca Magazine*, Cynthia related her first brush with artistic notoriety. "I entered an artistic competition in the *Liverpool Echo* newspaper. I drew a ballerina, sent it in and won a pound."

The Powell household was conspicuous by the interaction of Cynthia's parents who, she recalled in her book *John*, were the classic example of opposites attracting. "My father was easy going, kind, robust and jolly. My mother was unusual for her day. She had no interest in housework and she had a strong artistic streak They were opposites in many ways but they loved each other and I never heard them argue."

Cynthia was accepted to Junior Art Schoo*l* at age 12, a sure sign that Cynthia was destined for a career in the arts. But even at that age, Cynthia would admit to *Living on Mallorca* that her life goals were modest. "I never ever had a goal in life apart from wanting to do art and get my qualifications. I thought I'd take my teacher's diploma and teach."

Tragedy would strike about the time Cynthia turned 17. Her father had been in declining health for some time and eventually died of lung cancer. His dying words to his daughter would dash Cynthia's hopes when he told her that she would have to get a job to support her mother and that she would not be able to continue her art education in the prestigious Liverpool College of Art. The twin deaths of her father and her creative dreams would be short lived.

After Charles' passing, Lillian had other ideas. She was determined that her daughter would further her education and hatched a plan in which she would drag four single beds into the master bedroom of their house and rent them out to apprentice electricians with the extra money going toward her daughter's education.

In her book *John*, Cynthia recalled that the addition of the lodgers caused a change in the Powell way of life. "From then on, home was more like a boarding house. There were always queues for the bathroom and I had to get up at dawn if I wanted to be the first in. But I was hugely grateful to Mum and determined not to let her down."

Cynthia entered the Liverpool College of Art in September 1957. She was still in a state of mourning for her father but would admit in the book *John* that, "Art college gave me a new focus, something to be excited about, to work for and to take me out of our quiet little house of mourning into the world."

For Cynthia, that first year was cautious. She maintained a shy exterior, wore sensible, conservative clothes but settled seemingly easily into the world of higher education. "Well you go to art school and you try everything out first. You do what they call the foundation year and then you choose your potential. I would eventually go into commercial art and illustration," she related in a *Classicbands.com*. During that year she also had what would be considered her first real job, working part time at the cosmetics counter of a department store chain called Woolworths.

It was also during this 'coming out' that Cynthia fell in love for the first time. Barry was considered a prize among the girls. The son of a successful window cleaner, he was exotic looking and, at 22, he was a much more worldly man for the still impressionable 17 year-old Cynthia. They would be together for a year, seriously talking about getting engaged and, according to all reports, Cynthia was still a virgin. But as she recalled years later in her book *John*, he was persistent.

Cynthia would recall the first time she made love rather dispassionately in her book *John*. "One day he persuaded me to make love with him on the sofa in my parent's front room when my Mum was out. It took him hours to talk me into it, promising we would get married and telling me how much he loved me. When I finally agreed, I didn't think much of it. It was over in a flash and it was no fun. One day he announced that he had fallen for a girl who lived up the road. I was heartbroken. It was the first betrayal I had experienced and I vowed I'd never forgive him."

Cynthia would take Barry back some time later but the relationship would eventually fade. Going into her second year of college, Cynthia was coming out of her shell. She was dressing a bit more hip, she had changed her hairstyle and was becoming more sociable. She was now majoring in graphic arts and was taking a class in lettering as an adjunct.

It was during her first lettering class that Cynthia came face to face with John. And her initial reaction, recalled in *The Sun*, was that he was definitely not her type. "He was a real scruff, a real Teddy Boy who dressed in black and always had a guitar with him. He looked as if he would punch you just as soon as look at you. As soon as he walked into the class, you could tell he didn't want to be there."

But as she pointed out in a *Classicbands.com* conversation, John

Lennon was so alien to her way of thinking that she quickly found herself strangely drawn to him, often showing up early for class to stake out a seat in the area he normally sat and making a point of looking for him when she was out and about on campus. "He was a rebel. He was outrageous. He was something that I had not experienced before in my quite normal, straight-laced life. I was just instantly attracted to him."

They would begin somewhat of a ragged relationship. That they both wore glasses and were both fatherless was a jumping off point. Lennon grew to be good naturedly sarcastic whenever he saw her, teasing her with "Get you Miss Holylake," "Are you a nun?" or "Here comes Miss Prim." It was a rough and rugged give and take that Cynthia to her credit learned those were the ground rules if she wanted to be in Lennon's world. She was getting used to the idea that Lennon could be sarcastic and downright cruel. But it was that rebellious streak and the fact that he was so unlike any boy she had ever encountered that was driving her interest.

"I couldn't see him being interested in me," she recalled in her book *John*. "But that changed one day when I was packing my things in class and John was sitting a few feet away with his guitar. Suddenly he began to play 'Ain't She Sweet.' I blushed scarlet, made an excuse and fled before the end of the song. But I'd seen that look in his eyes. Could it be that John fancied me too?"

Lennon and Cynthia would continue to circle each other emotionally for some time, Cynthia hoping against hope that something with Lennon could be possible while the college misfit was giving mixed signals to Cynthia while gathering steam and popularity on the local club circuit as part of The Quarrymen. An end of the semester party in 1958 would tell the tale.

Cynthia was looking forward to the semester break and, on a subconscious level, hoping that the time away would allow her to get over Lennon. Lennon showed up at the party and immediately came over to Cynthia and asked her to dance, as was chronicled in the book *John*. Lennon screamed out mid dance with "Do you fancy going out with me?"

Cynthia took that moment to stammer out that she was engaged. Lennon did not take it well and shot back with "I didn't ask you to fucking marry me did I?" before walking away. She knew she had made a mistake and would spend the rest of the party sulking. As the party was breaking up, John came over to Cynthia and asked if she wanted to go to a pub with some people. In his own way, Cynthia knew that Lennon was giving her another chance. "I knew I was hooked," she would later recall in the book *John*. "I was staying."

At the pub, Cynthia would be… well rather unCynthia like, having quite a few drinks and relishing the pub's loud and raucous vibe. At one point, the couple slipped away from the crowd and out into the night where he and Cynthia kissed long and passionately before Lennon whispered in her ear that his friend had a room not too far away that they could go to. Cynthia said yes.

"We couldn't have cared less about the mess in the room and headed for the mattress, where we made love for the next hour," she said in the book *John*. "For me it was special and very different and I think it was equally special for John."

Their love now officially consummated, Cynthia and John made a mad dash for the last train that would take her home. After one last kiss, Cynthia jumped on the train. John yelled out ``What are you doing tomorrow and the next day and the next?"

"Seeing you," she recalled shouting back.

Cynthia was suddenly in a relationship that she did not quite understand. But even while hopelessly in love, she was candid in telling *Classicrockbands.com* that she was not thinking beyond those early emotions. "You know something, when you're very young, love is very blind. I had no thoughts of the future. I had no idea what was going to happen. We were living for the moment and that's the way it should have been and it was. So I didn't know."

When she was not in school, she was always with John. It was idyllic from the word go but it was also a bumpy romance. Cynthia was learning on the job so to speak when it came to her lover. She knew enough about Lennon's early years to know that they were marked with trauma, tragedy and emotional highs and lows. "During our college, John was very insecure," Cynthia told author Chris Hunt in *Uncut Legends*. " He was very raw inside and full of pain, emotional pain. I think he really relied on me, and he kept testing me to make sure I was constant and that I wouldn't do anything to hurt or harm him."

As the relationship evolved. She was aware that he could become angry, especially when he had been drinking and that he was prone to fits of jealousy and possessiveness. But it would take a day at art school when Lennon totally lost his mind that Cynthia discovered that her lover could

11

become violent at a moment's notice. On the day in question, Cynthia was dancing with a mutual friend, Stuart Sutcliffe, when Lennon walked in, saw them dancing and immediately jumped to the wrong conclusion.

Cynthia's memories of the violent encounter that followed would be widely reported in later years by numerous outlets including *The Sun*. "Out of nowhere he just smacked me across the face and I hit my head against a pipe." Cynthia dumped Lennon on the spot. The pair would remain apart for three months before Lennon would call out of the blue and beg Cynthia to take him back. "He was desperately sorry. It was just an instant and he couldn't help himself. He didn't do it again and I wouldn't have been with him if he had. It was the first and last time he lifted a finger to me."

Cynthia would have a front row seat of history in the making as The Quarrymen morphed into Johnny and the Moondogs to The Silver Beatles and finally to The Beatles. For Cynthia, those early gigs reflected on the ease of Lennon and her relationship. She was well known to be with Lennon and, through a vague sense of either possessiveness on the part of the band members and their women, it was never an issue with Cynthia going where her man was working. Her first trip to Hamburg in 1960 would be a real eye opener as she recalled in *Classicbands.com*.

"Hamburg was very violent and very dangerous. But the band had made friends with some locals on a previous trip, most notably Astrid Kirchherr and Klaus Voormann, who knew the ropes. So when I went, I was well protected. I had no problems. The area where the band was playing was very rough and rugged. There were drugs and lots of murders. Sounds good, doesn't it?"

Cynthia also came to know the reality of a band that, while growing in popularity, was still a struggling band and, at the end of the day, still pretty much poor and penniless. "I'd seen them in all sorts of situations, ridiculous places," she recalled in *Classicbands.com* ``They were trying to earn a crust, just earn some money."

Fate would take a hand in 1961 when a local record shop owner, Brian Epstein, caught a performance by the then Beatles and offered to manage them. Long story short, Epstein was a hustler who knew people and it wasn't long before Beatles demos were being sent around to major labels.

It was at that time, when things were the most chaotic and exciting, that Cynthia discovered that she was pregnant.

Cynthia had often acknowledged to a highly active and spontaneous sex life, often conducted in alleys and doorways, and that birth control had never been a thought. "I wasn't even thinking about the future," she proclaimed in *Classicbands.com*. "I lived for the moment. I was never really dreaming about the future or marriage or babies. It never entered my mind. I was just very happy to be with him. I'm quite a survivor so probably inside me I thought 'well, I can probably survive whatever happens.'"

In the book *Lennon* by veteran music journalist Ray Coleman, Cynthia would elaborate on the fact that she and John were both babes in the woods when it came to the consequences of unprotected sex. "There was no planning. There was no pill in those days. We considered nothing except ourselves and didn't consider the consequences. Neither John nor I ever gave pregnancy a thought. We weren't thinking about anything like prevention."

It would be with that "whatever happens" attitude in place that Cynthia would break the news to Lennon in August 1962. As described in the book *Lennon*, Lennon came around for a visit and found Cynthia uncharacteristically quiet and withdrawn. He asked what was the matter. Cynthia said in *Lennon* what happened next. "I told him 'No it's not okay. I'm pregnant. That's what's the matter.'" Cynthia recalled that John was in a panic. But once the panic subsided, John became unexpectedly practical and conservative when he told Cynthia, "Don't worry Cyn. We'll get married."

Lennon was of two minds at the news. He was a by-product of a time when if a boy got a girl pregnant, they got married. But if he had his druthers, he would not have married Cynthia. The Beatles were on the verge of exploding on the music scene with the release of their single 'Love Me Do' and for Lennon, truth be told, Cynthia being pregnant and the prospect of being married was often taking second place to The Beatles' coming success. And Cynthia was of like mind when she offered in the book *Lennon* "He wasn't ready to settle down. He wasn't any more ready for a child than I was. He was committed to it while it had to be done but he'd want to be moving on to the next thing real fast."

The young couple did not know which end was up and so they turned to Brian Epstein to make the arrangements. In due course, he had arranged a wedding license and set the date of August 23, 1962 for the ceremony at the Mount Pleasant Register Office in Liverpool. At the time, Cynthia was five months pregnant. The ceremony was sparsely attended by Lennon's bandmates Paul McCartney and George Harrison, their manager Epstein and Cynthia's brother and his wife. Cynthia would remember the surreal nature of that day in *The Sun*.

"There was no photographer. We don't even have a photo from the day and the guy who married us looked like he was doing a funeral, never mind a marriage. Outside the window was this guy with a pneumatic drill who was drilling throughout the ceremony (which lasted all of three minutes). The whole experience was naïve, innocent, bizarre but beautiful. All the Beatles had suits on and I can still see them looking panic stricken. It was just weird and it was pouring rain. Afterward we all went to a place called Recee's Café for the wedding lunch. It was the meal of the day, soup, roast chicken and trifle. We drank water and lemonade because the place didn't have a wine license."

That would conclude Cynthia's 'special day.'

The Beatles had a show to play that night and so Cynthia would spend her wedding night alone. Being alone was something Cynthia would become accustomed to in the coming months. With Epstein guiding their fortunes, The Beatles, largely on the strength of their first two singles 'Love Me Do' and 'Please Please Me' and constant touring, Lennon was rarely around. Cynthia was okay with the situation, knowing full well that becoming famous was hard work. But three months into her pregnancy, Cynthia was not feeling right and thought she might be having a miscarriage and her first thoughts were for her husband.

"I was alone, John was away and I started panicking." She revealed in the book *Lennon*. Fears of a miscarriage proved to be a false alarm, requiring only a couple of days of bed rest. "When John came home I told him about it and told him I was particularly frightened while I was pregnant because if I had lost the baby, there would have been nobody to help me." The incident would prove pivotal in that it would force a reconciliation between Lennon and his Aunt Mimi who had bad-mouthed the couple for months and was a no-show at the wedding. It turned out that Mimi had softened with the marriage and offered to let Cynthia live with her.

Life for a pop band, especially one with four handsome young men and a target fan base that was largely young and female, was as much image as it was talent and Epstein was readily aware that the right image could make the band and any hint of turn off could break them Epstein's notion that if word got out that Lennon was not only married but that his wife was pregnant would mar the notion of availability in their fans. And so Cynthia would recall that Epstein would lay down the law and that she was quick to fall in line with the deception.

"If the main man in the group, John, was found to be married, then it might take away from that success," she related in a *National Public Radio* interview. "So I walked around pregnant for quite a long time, hiding it. I'd wear these big, blousy clothes. I was asked many times if I was John's wife and I had to refuse, saying 'no, no I'm somebody else.'"

And in a sense, she had, in a literal sense, truly become somebody else.

Her hopes to get an art teaching degree and, as she often stated, be able to support their lives until The Beatles became profitable went by the wayside in the vortex that was the pregnancy, the marriage and the rapid rise of The Beatles. She had been so distracted that when she took her teaching exams, she failed them and never looked back. "My talents and aspirations had to be put on the back burner," she reflected in a *BBC News* interview. "But that was as much my fault as anybody else's."

Years later, Cynthia would be more direct in discussing the matter with *Hello Magazine*. "His career started and mine finished. If I hadn't met John and got married I would have been an art school teacher or gone into the commercial art world."

Cynthia would spend the last four months of her pregnancy alone. The Beatles were on the road constantly at that point, capitalizing on two hit singles and a growing mania for the band. John would call regularly to check on Cynthia but while keeping in touch was nice, it was not the same as having Lennon being around. But Cynthia would be pretty level headed about his absence. She had known the consequences of stardom and was more than willing to play her role.

John Charles Julian Lennon was born on April 8, 1963. Cynthia had to endure the rigors of childbirth alone as The Beatles were in the midst of an extensive British tour. And as she recalled in the book *Lennon*, it had not been an easy birth. "I was something like three days in the hospital before Julian arrived. And then he had jaundice, the umbilical cord was around his neck and he had a large mole on his head. He had to be left alone for 24 hours. I couldn't touch him. I was petrified. But I was scared more than anything about the birthmark, the mole. Knowing John's horror of deformities, I was absolutely panic stricken about what John's reaction would be."

Lennon's reaction to the birthmark was that it didn't matter. But

Cynthia's paranoia was so extreme at the time that for a number of days she put a hat on Julian's head so that Lennon would not continue to notice the blemish.

For the remainder of 1963, Cynthia was the proverbial stay-at-home mother, her hands full with the care and feeding of Julian while The Beatles were touring, recording and playing pop music's newest next big thing. Although occasionally bored, Cynthia had taken quite well to her new role in life, although she would often wish that Lennon was around more. In early 1964, Lennon, admittedly totally out of character for the usually self-centered musician, would surprise Cynthia with an offer she could not refuse.

The Beatles were about to embark on their very first American tour that would include the all important appearances on the publicity bonanza that was *The Ed Sullivan Show* and the first vestiges of how Beatlemania was making its way to America. It had long been an edict within the band that girlfriends and wives were not permitted on tour or in the studio. But Lennon chose to make an exception.

"Well I was allowed to go on that first tour," Cynthia recalled in a *National Public Radio* interview. And I do mean allowed. I didn't ask John. I think John wanted me to go because it was so exciting to come to America for the first time. I'd never been to America and it was a treat for me. It was really a fantastic experience. But that was enough. I wouldn't have wanted to have done it again. It was just too much."

The reality of that tour would prove an eye opener for Cynthia. She was immediately drawn in by the excitement of it all. The hotels, the food and getting to see the sights in a part of the world she had never experienced. But as she remembered during the *National Public Radio* interview, she also got to see the down side of stardom and adulation. "All we saw was the inside of hotel rooms, the inside of Cadillacs. We were surrounded by mounted police on one occasion, motorbike escorts on another occasion, we were constantly trying to escape from hotels and the screaming fans. It was all quite horrendous, apart from the actual performances, which were fantastic. The rest of it was horrendous because you couldn't see beyond the prison that you were in at that particular time."

Cynthia would sense during the tour that the women in their men's lives would often be an afterthought as The Beatles interacted with women on the tour. A lot of it was harmless fun as they were constantly being mobbed by female fans, screaming their lungs out for their favorite as they battled it out among the bemused Beatles for an autograph, a photo or a touch that would send them into spasms of hysteria. Cynthia could deal with that level of adulation. But at one point in the '64 tour she was up close and personal with a deeper and much more primal situation.

It was during a stay in New York that The Beatles and entourage were invited to the suite of noted disc jockey Murray The K. "And in the room there were all of these draped beautiful ladies," Cynthia told *National Public Radio*. "Five beautiful ladies all draped around. And we all walked in and looked at them and looked at each other and wondered what on earth we were supposed to do in a situation like this. Because it was obvious what they were there for. And of course I was the fly in the ointment because I was the wife of one of The Beatles. So it was embarrassing for them and embarrassing for me. I realized at that point what it was going to be like in the future. Just women throwing themselves at them the whole time."

With the sudden and massive impact of The Beatles, Cynthia would find herself dealing with two distinct lifestyles, motherhood and the sudden impact of unbridled celebrity. Cynthia would acknowledge that Lennon and she would occasionally go away on holiday but the overriding elements in Cynthia's life had boiled down to motherhood and The Beatles. And then there was the question of money and the notion of suddenly being thrust from being poor to money being of no object.

"We were like children in a world of a lot of money," she told *Hello*. "We didn't have to pay any bills, it was all done by money men and accountants. John did not carry money around with him. He rarely signed a check."

Nevertheless, the couple would grow accustomed to the sudden wealth and would spring for one very expensive bobble in 1964. "The first thing you do if you're a pop star and you get a lot of money, you buy a mansion. That takes you from one extreme in life to another," she offered to *National Public Radio*. If it had been up to Lennon, they would have settled on something pricy but hip in the big city. But Cynthia was feeling the need for isolation and a degree of security as a new mother, insisted that they had to buy a place out in the country. Lennon would agree and the couple soon signed on the dotted line to buy a mansion in the toney, upper class conservative city of Weybridge, some 20 miles outside of London.

When Lennon was off the road or away from the studio, he could be quite the handyman, putting up curtains and puttering around the property, often with the assistance of his bandmate George Harrison. But, for the most part, Cynthia was often in a state of shock and often alone in the big, rambling house as John was often away, with the day to day issues of the day falling on her. "All of a sudden You find yourself the chauffeur, and the housekeeper and the cook and the interior designer and all the things in life that you never experienced before and that you weren't brought up to do," she sighed in an interview with *National Public Radio*. "I was left to cope with and handle all of it which was hard work. It was a full time job, actually."

It was at this point that Cynthia's influence and importance in the life of Lennon and, by association, The Beatles began to take more prominence and importance. On the surface, she had been dismissed as wife and mother, both important elements in any relationship. But as the craziness of Beatlemania began to unfold, Cynthia's quiet strength, keeping the home fires burning while juggling motherhood and an unpredictable spouse became more obvious. In many circles, she would come to be known as the person who kept Lennon, emotionally, from going off the rails.

Not surprisingly, Cynthia was calm and to the point when assessing her own importance and influence in *The Express* when she offered "I was looking after his interests in my own little way, caring about his future and hoping he was happy because he had to go through so much hell to do what he did."

And what she would come to find out was that, even when Lennon was home, he was never really there, which played havoc with Cynthia's notion of what a normal family dynamic should be as she explained to *National Public Radio*. "He [John] used to sleep an awful lot. And he would wake up when we were ready to go to bed, if you know what I mean. With a small child, you have to be up early in the morning and then you're pretty exhausted at night, whereas John's hours changed. He'd be up at night and then in bed during the day. So the whole fabric of our life changed because of the work he was doing and because of the pressures from outside."

In later years, Cynthia would often embellish or clarify the state of their marriage, in some cases putting a positive spin on it as was the case in the quote from the website *InMyWriteMind.com*. "As far as the marriage was concerned, we got on great. It wasn't the greatest whizzo active relationship and once he [Lennon] became a Beatle we didn't go out as husband and wife. But we were strong in the unit at home."

While she understood the pressures of stardom, the one thing that continued to concern her was her husband's fidelity. The Beatles were on the road and for long periods of time. She assumed that her husband would get lonely and tempted. It was a situation that was confirmed one day in conversation with long time roadie Mal Evans. Evans was candid in saying that there were always women around and that the boys would often go off with them. "He said 'I'm not going to give you details but it happened all the time,'" she related in *InMyWriteMind.com*. "He said 'All pop stars need it. They need women. They go out, find good looking ones and bring them up.'" Cynthia was not necessarily shocked at the news. "I wasn't that stupid to know that when the boys were on the road anything could happen."

There was resignation and disappointment at the news but Cynthia had a logical streak about her that allowed her to weather the storm. "I had blind faith," she admitted in the book *Lennon*. "I couldn't imagine John being involved with another woman. And even if I had, I would have ignored it because he always came back. Whatever John did outside our marriage, he didn't flaunt anything. So when I learned later about the temptations he had succumbed to, I had the satisfaction of knowing he had protected me."

Cynthia's declaration was noble but it was a sign that the reality of their marriage was in jeopardy. Lennon's rebellious nature had made him a prime target for the excesses of stardom. He had evolved into a heavy drinker and drug user which would lead to both violent emotional outbursts and moments of psychological withdrawal. Cynthia had sensed that their relationship was changing, often more than roommates and friends than loving husband and wife. Cynthia was often blinded by the uncertainty and unpredictability of Lennon.

In 1967, she would be forced to deal with it head on.

Cynthia was washing dishes one day when Lennon came up behind her, put his arms around her waist and blurted out "I want to get if off my chest Cyn. There have been hundreds of other women."

Cynthia would recall her reaction in the book *Lennon*. "Strangely it was a very loving moment. I was in tears, not in anger or shock but tears of happiness that he could tell me that we once again got close enough for him to get rid of it, talk it through and put it on a different level. Perhaps it would have all come down better if I had been able to be a bit more aggressive. But I was so happy that at last he felt he could open his heart and tell me what was on his mind."

But even with this seeming comeback in their relationship, Cynthia, ever the realist, felt in her heart and soul that the marriage would not last and she put the blame, in a philosophical sense, on the fact that they were growing apart. "I guess it was my boring, down to earth attitude that probably sent John running," she said in *InMyWriteMind.com*. "I see things in black and white rather than in grey or colors. It's just my upbringing. I'm a realist."

And being a realist, Cynthia most certainly sensed that Lennon's 'confession' must have been a smokescreen to the fact that, as early as 1965, he was already seeing somebody on the sly. Avante garde artist Yoko Ono.

Reports tend to differ but Ono seems to have entered the Lennon universe when she approached Paul McCartney about the possibility of using written copies of some of their songs in an upcoming project. Lennon and Ono would, according to one report, come face to face at an exhibition of Ono's work. Lennon seemed alternately amused and cynical about Ono's artistic talents but found her intensity and sincerity of interest. They would begin an active correspondence as their mutual attraction grew. Phone calls would follow and then Ono began to unexpectedly drop by and leave things for Lennon.

But Cynthia would insist that she did not believe there was anything to be concerned about. "I had no idea whatsoever that there was any kind of relationship going on," she told interviewer Chris Hunt in *Uncut Legends*. "I thought there might have been some artistic connection, but not in any way an emotional relationship or an affair. My staff didn't tell me anything. I had a housekeeper and all she did was tell me was that Yoko would come to the house and leave things behind for John. That didn't mean anything to me because there were lots of fans who came to the house."

But after a time, Cynthia's feminine intuition came to the fore and a level of reality set in. "You knew that something was going to happen and only you know because of your sensitivity and knowledge of the person you've been living with for 10 years," she told *National Public Radio*. " You know exactly what's going to happen. As far as Yoko is concerned, I knew there was not a thing I could do about it, any more than there was anything I could do about John taking drugs at the time. There was no way I could have stopped him."

Things would remain tense. There was the much-publicized Transcendental Medication journey in which Cynthia would miss the train and Lennon left without her. For Cynthia, it was a sign that things were getting dire, especially after Cynthia arrived on her own at the seminar, only to spend the entire time either being berated or ignored. Consequently, it would be an almost welcome break when, upon returning to England, John suggested that Cynthia and Julian should take a holiday in Greece while Lennon remained behind to write songs for what would be the *White Album*. Cynthia liked the idea and felt, with the marriage hanging by a thread, separation might, indeed, make the heart grow fonder.

"We both needed space to breathe," she acknowledged in the book *Lennon*. "I don't think he was intentionally getting rid of me. He just wanted to sort himself out, just as I did."

As it turned out, the vacation in Greece had, emotionally, done Cynthia a lot of good. She was refreshed, optimistic with the idea that the time apart would rejuvenate her marriage and life with Lennon. Cynthia would come home early in high spirits as she entered her home... only to come upon Lennon and Ono sitting in robes and kimonos, calmly sipping tea and obviously having spent the night together. Various reports, including one from *The Independent*, from that period indicated that the pair had spent the night recording songs for what would become the album *Two Virgins* and then made love. When Lennon spotted Cynthia he calmly said "Oh hi." Ono just smiled and then turned her back to her.

In the book *Lennon*, Cynthia recalled that moment in emotional detail. "It was like walking into a brick wall. It was as if I didn't belong anymore. I suppose I should have been prepared for it but I wasn't. I wasn't angry at the vision. I was just shattered."

Years later in quotes from *National Public Radio* and *The Express*, Cynthia seemed almost matter of fact in recalling the moment. "She had been staying the night with John and I came home and there they were. Which was sort of curtains for our marriage."

But surprisingly, Lennon was warm and encouraging to Cynthia, claiming that the sexual encounter was only intellectual in nature. For several weeks Cynthia was torn, on the one hand believing the marriage was over while still holding out hope that their marriage could be saved. It was under a cloud of sadness and uncertainty that she went ahead with plans to take her mother and son on a holiday in Italy. It was a few days into the vacation in Italy that an associate of Lennon's showed up with a message. Lennon was going to divorce Cynthia on the grounds of adultery, and take custody of Julian. Cynthia knew the adultery charge was a lie.

As the long and painful divorce proceedings played out in the courts through and in the press and complicated by Ono's pregnancy and subsequent miscarriage of Lennon's child during that period, Cynthia was left to contemplate what had happened to the man she once loved. In a quote from the website *CynthiaLennonQuotes.com*.

"I knew the man up until our divorce. After that, I didn't know the man at all. I worried about the complete change I saw in him. He lost his sense of humor and he got aggressive. He wasn't for the world anymore. He was just for Yoko. Before that, he opened his arms and embraced the world with his wit and his humor. After he met Yoko he was a completely different kind of person."

The divorce decree was filed November 8, 1968. Cynthia would receive a lump sum settlement, child support and a trust fund for Julian that would be made available when Lennon's son was 21. She would describe in her book *John* how her day in court was a terrifying emotional ordeal. "I was summoned to the divorce court and I went alone. Walking into the court was terrifying. The place was packed with the press and I had to swear in front of them under oath that my marriage had broken down, that my husband had publicly admitted adultery and that Yoko was pregnant by him."

Cynthia was officially on her own and was not sure what to do next.

Ten years as the wife of John Lennon had accustomed her to a certain way of life that was, with the thud of a judge's gavel, no longer hers. "Throughout this awful surreal experience, I felt humiliated and painfully aware that I was alone," she reflected in her book *John*. "Afterward, I fled home and collapsed sick with apprehension about the future. I had no idea how I would cope."

But with a child to raise and a sense of notoriety that, whether she liked it or not, would always follow her, Cynthia set out to make her way as a single woman. Initially, it was a time of reflection and falling back on elements of her conservative, straightforward, familial attitudes to keep her moving forward after the trauma of the divorce from Lennon.

"I was emotionally bereft," she offered in *The Independent*.

"Financially, I was comfortable but, as with all traumas, you find solace from family and friends and, to be honest, you just have to muddle through, get on with it and, for the sake of the innocent party, your child, keep your feet on the ground."

And a big first step to that new beginning was to go back to using her maiden name Powell.

One thing Cynthia soon discovered was that once the divorce from Lennon was final, all contact with any person remotely connected to The Beatles stopped, a sign that she was now personae non grata to people she had known for years. With one exception. Paul McCartney.

McCartney had formed a seemingly enduring friendship with Cynthia over the years and sensed that she would now be ostracized from the Beatles clique. But that was not his way. And so one afternoon Cynthia was surprised when there was a knock on the door and McCartney was standing there. He was there as a friend, checking on Cynthia and Julian's well-being and he had come with a gift of sorts. On the drive to Cynthia's house, inspiration had hit and McCartney began writing a song entitled 'Hey Jules,' a heartfelt tune designed to brighten Julian's mood. It was a song that would eventually be renamed 'Hey Jude' and would go on to become a classic. In later years Cynthia would often recall that day and 'how I was touched by his obvious concern for our welfare.'"

Cynthia would quickly round into getting along in this post Beatle world and would soon find herself back on the dating scene, in particular dating an Italian hotel owner named Roberto Bassanini. Cynthia was looking for love and a love that was the polar opposite of what she had experienced. The romance moved quickly and the couple were married in 1970. "Roberto was like a breath of fresh air," Cynthia recalled in *The Independent*. "After my very public divorce, his family welcomed us with open arms. The contrast was like a sunny day in Italy compared to a hoary frost in Moscow."

Unfortunately, the marriage to Bassanini would soon founder and the couple divorced in 1973. Once again alone and with an income that she acknowledged in *People* "was never stable," she cast about for different ways of making a living. Cynthia tentatively returned to her first passion, art, and while it was creatively satisfying, it was not commercially successful. She would have modest luck with a bed and breakfast/ restaurant called *Oliver's Bistro*. Nineteen seventy-eight found Cynthia once again in love and married to engineer John Twist.

23

That same year, seemingly constantly in need of money, Cynthia succumbed to the temptation to exploit her life with Lennon when she wrote *A Twist of Lennon*, a memoir of her time with John. By all accounts *A Twist of Lennon* was a straightforward account of her life with Lennon, alternately forthright and honest in chronicling the ups and downs of their life together. For his part, Lennon was not thrilled with his ex-wife writing a tell-all and tried to stop the book from being published. His efforts failed and the book came out. Reviews were mixed and many saw it as Cynthia's internal battle of trying to forge her own life away from Beatlemania while, at the same time, seeing a commercial opportunity in telling her side of the story.

Cynthia would remain out of the spotlight for the next two years, doing the occasional interview to promote *A Twist of Lennon* or, when she was in the right frame of mind, the odd media interview that would focus on living with Lennon. She would be straightforward and, by degrees, forthcoming, having repeated her Lennon anecdotes so often that they had become literal mental script pages she would trot out for the inevitable questions. But she readily admitted to *People* that while the years away from Lennon had changed her some, some things have remained the same.

"I don't want to forget John, nor should I. All my memories are intact. But the past is over now."

On December 8, 1980, John Lennon was shot and killed by an obsessed fan on the streets of New York. Two hours later the phone rang at Cynthia's home. It was Ringo with the news. "The memory of Ringo's words, crackling over the transatlantic line were crystal clear," she painfully recounted to the *BBC News*. "'Cynthia, I'm sorry. John's dead.' At that moment, I had only one thought and that was to get back to Wales to tell Julian about his father's death."

Cynthia would continue on with her life and in what had quickly turned into a troublesome third marriage that would end when she and Twist divorced in 1982. It was at that point that Cynthia discovered a pattern in her love life and her economic life that was taking her on a seemingly never-ending journey to the poorhouse as she admitted in conversation with the *Sun Times*. "Apart from John, the men I have fallen in love with have never been good at earning a living. "I'm afraid all the men in my life were much more interested in exploiting my Lennon Legacy than I ever was. It was always 'why don't you write a book or why don't you do this or that?' I was very open to their suggestions because I was vulnerable. I needed the money. I had to earn a living somehow."

Cynthia's next romantic relationship would take a slightly different course. Jim Christie was Cynthia's chauffeur and while the relationship, which would last 17 years without resulting in marriage, proved to be quite a natural fit. "Jim had never felt he was living in John Lennon's shadow," she said in a *Merseyworld.com* interview. "He was four years younger than me and wasn't really part of the Beatle scene. He knew Julian before he knew me and, in fact, taught Julian to ride motorbikes. We became friends as a result. He slotted so easily into my life. It was really a miracle for me."

Cynthia was adamant that another marriage was far from her mind, as was Christie's, and once Julian was on board with their non-traditional relationship, Cynthia remained confident in her new romantic situation as she acknowledged in *JohnAndCynthiaLennon.blogspot.com*. "We're not married and we're not planning on getting married. Jim and I are partners. We live together, work together and we have a stronger relationship than any marriage. We've reached a time in our lives when we don't need to get married. We feel right as we are."

In 1985, Cynthia and Jim relocated to the small northwestern English town of Cumbria, a largely rural, by degrees isolated, hamlet, all of which suited Cynthia to a T. "We moved to Cumbria to escape being at the end of the phone," she told *JohnAndCynthia blogspot.com*. "When anything was about The Beatles, I was always being pursued or harassed. I was getting really fed up with it."

With the death of Lennon, *A Twist of Lennon*, which had been a modest but ultimately unspectacular seller, suddenly spiked, going into a second and third printing and ultimately selling in excess of 200,000 copies. Cynthia saw the reality of her life—whether she liked it or not, she was a significant part of Beatle history and, as crass as it seemed, there was a living to be made off her connection. And the way to do that was to return to using Lennon as her last name. Cynthia was being highly pragmatic on going back to her married name in an interview with *The Independent*.

"Do you imagine I would have been awarded a three year contract to design bedding and textiles (with *Vantona Vyella* in 1983) with the name Powell? Neither did they. When it is necessary to earn a living, it is necessary to bite the bullet and take the flack."

One element of Cynthia's post-divorce lifestyle was that she was constantly on the move, changing addresses and even countries of residence. To many observers, it was as if Cynthia was running away from something. But in conversation with *Merseyworld.com*, she would make a point of indicating that she was actually running toward peace of mind. "After John and I split up, I seemed to be constantly on the movie. I would move from house to house just about every three years which, in a way, was ridiculous for so many different reasons. But for me, it made perfect sense. It was all about being on some kind of inner search for peace."

Cynthia would begin what would be nearly two decades of making money off her Beatle connection by selling off *Oliver's Bistro*. Then it was on to what many would consider mercenary pursuits. In 1988, Cynthia created a perfume line called *Woman* (named after the John Lennon song) which was short-lived. The following year she returned to the restaurant business with a kitschy eatery called *Lennon's* which also failed.

Depending on who one talked to, Cynthia, while not destitute, did need money and quite a bit of it. With poverty once again staring her in the face, Cynthia made a decision that had long been an option but one she had, subconsciously, fought against. On August 29, 1991, Cynthia's memorabilia from her days with Lennon went on the auction block at Christie's auction house. Among the items that would go under the gavel for an estimated $100,000 were personal letters from Lennon to Cynthia, a drawing done by Lennon during an LSD trip and a vinyl acetate of the song 'Lucy In The Sky With Diamonds.'

Cynthia was of two minds when it came to auctioning off the personal mementos. She told *People* that "I've enjoyed these things for 30 years. But it was time for a change." She was a bit more mercenary when addressing the auction of deeply personal belongings when she offered *The Independent*. "I think in life we collect so much baggage, when you have a clear out, you send things to a car boot sale. My baggage was in demand and sold at Christie's. When you have to pay bills, you're not proud and you certainly can't take it with you."

Easily one of the more unusual attempts to make money came when, in 1995, she attempted to become a pop star, aided and abetted by old friend McCartney as producer and with a bit of acoustic guitar, singing a cover of the classic Mary Hopkins hit "Those Were The Days."

"The last time I sang in front of an audience was when I was in the Holylake parish girl's choir," she laughingly recalled in *Merseyworld.com*. "I haven't had the occasion to sing from that day to this but even though my friends sniffed a bit when I told them I was making a record, they ate their words when they heard it."

Unfortunately, all the inherent hype in the world could not prevent Cynthia's pop debut from failing to chart.

Her run of bad luck would continue in 1998 when, after a seemingly idyllic 17-year relationship, her partner Christie simply packed his belongings one day and moved out. Saddened but unbowed, Cynthia simply moved on and once again succumbed to the fairly easy money offered by the numerous Beatle conventions and festivals that would pay her handsomely to simply talk about her life with Lennon and sign some autographs. Her appearances would last for some years but by the mid 90's she had begun to tire of making her living off of a past life. When she finally called her convention days over, in both *The Independent* and *People*, she acknowledged the good and bad of the experience.

"The Beatle fans have always been wonderful to me and I think I have reciprocated. But I do believe there is life for me after The Beatles and all I can say is it's my life and it's time I put it in order. I'd had enough. I thought 'Do I want to be wheeled onto television programs in a wheelchair at 70, discussing The Beatles and John?' I just couldn't face it anymore."

Now free to concentrate on her art, Cynthia had rounded into a later in life with a sense of freedom and confidence. She was in a good place that had seemingly survived the end of her relationship with Christie, so much so that, in 2002, she met and married nightclub owner Noel Charles, a friend of Julian's. It seemed a good match for her fourth trip to the altar. Charles was older, settled and secure and was somebody who would give Cynthia a solid relationship with nary a hint of her Beatle past in play. The couple moved to Majorca Spain, where, in 2005, Cynthia wrote what many perceived as a more mature memoir of life with and after John Lennon, entitled simply *John*.

John was successful on the commercial front but would walk the line critically. There were already a lot of books on the Beatles and, in particular, on Lennon. A lot of ground had been covered over the years and while *John* was interesting, it went over a lot of familiar territory. Cynthia made a spirited defense to that charge in an interview with *HeralExtra.com*. "This is my book, my experience and, if it's not the same as everybody else's, that's fair game. I have to speak from my point of view and my feelings about the whole story."

One particular poignant moment in John was Cynthia's declaration that if she had known as a teenager where falling in love with Lennon would lead, she never would have taken the plunge. "I didn't really mean it as so final as that," she clarified to *HeraldExtra.com*. "It's such a double-edged feeling. When I say that if I had known what was ahead of me I'd have walked the other way, well obviously I couldn't and wouldn't and didn't. I didn't take the easy path."

Cynthia's time with Charles would be peaceful. He was a natural born protector and was always with her during media interviews and when they were out and about. He was offering Cynthia the most sense of comfort and being she had experienced in years. Noel Charles died of cancer on March 11, 2013.

Cynthia shared her thoughts on his death some 18 months later in what would reportedly be her last interview, a conversation with *Celebrities In Majorca* magazine. "When I lost Noel, my brain was all over the place. The pain never goes, that's all I can say. It can last for just half an hour, an hour or two hours. At this particular point I am content. In a tragic and logical way, all of a sudden I have the space to start again."

Less than a year later, Cynthia would die after a short bout with cancer on April 1, 2015 with Julian at her side. Her passing brought condolences from the likes of former Beatles McCartney and Starr as well as a seemingly forced acknowledgement from Ono. It would remain for her soon Julian, on his website *JulianLennon.com* to memorialize his mother as only a loving son could.

You gave your life for me
You gave your life for love
The feeling still remains
Though you're on a different plane
Your world is full of angels
You've become one
With God above you're free

Chapter Two
Maureen Starkey

If there is a Beatle wives equivalent of Rodney Dangerfield's "I can't get no respect," the mantle would clearly fall hard on Maureen Starkey.

To historians, Maureen was the classic example of a girl with no drive, no discernible ambition and no real goals who got real lucky and married a Beatle. Perhaps the assessment is a bit harsh. But there is much evidence in the telling that Maureen was, indeed, at the right place at the right time.

"Being a mother and being happily married is just about as much as any girl can ask for," Maureen was quoted as saying regarding the ambition front in *WattpadW.com*.

Even Ringo Starr, who married Maureen, was damning with faint praise in a *Beatlestory.com* story when he acknowledged, "She's just sort of ordinary. She's from Liverpool."

Former Beatles press officer Tony Barrow offered in *US News* an equally blunt assessment, offering that Maureen was less glamorous, less famous and not nearly as smart as other members of The Beatles Wives Club. But on the up side "she was chirpy with an irreverent sense of humor."

But others would equally acknowledge that Maureen was indeed a salt of the earth girl, level-headed, caring and giving who was quick to speak her mind and was always fashionably dressed. In her book *Wonderful Tonight*, former Beatle wife Pattie Boyd would describe Maureen this way, "She was jolly, friendly and relaxed."

Beatle insider at the time and author Chris O'Dell was definitely in Maureen's corner when she offered in *US News* that, "She was a character who got along with everyone. She wasn't afraid to be her own person. She dressed the way she wanted to and she spoke the way she wanted to. Her loyalty was one of her deepest qualities."

As was her desire to remain above the Beatlemania fray and well behind the scenes. Maureen always valued her privacy and, to be candid, abhorred the media, saying as much when her honeymoon with Ringo was interrupted when the press descended on the newly married couple. "I don't like reporters and things," she told the press in a transcript chronicled by *Beatleinterviews.org*.

Mary Cox was born on August 4, 1946 in Liverpool, Merseyside, the only child of ship steward Joseph Cox and his wife Florence. Maureen's early years mirrored her working class roots and the so-called 'rough parts' of her neighborhood. Although her upbringing was fairly strict and conservative to the point that she spent her formative years in a local convent school, Maureen was, from the onset, anything but a good girl. She was street smart and was known to have a bit of a mouth on her, often letting loose with such bon mots as "bloody hell," "sodden hellfire" and "it's breaking my brain" according to the *BornLate.blogspot*.

As she grew into her teens, her wild child tendencies were becoming more evident. She would constantly defy the school's dress code by turning her school uniform around to make it look like a frock. In an attempt to look cool, Maureen would give a school friend 10 cigarettes a day to teach her how to hold and smoke a cigarette properly. What Maureen was up to would inevitably get back to her parents who, given their own conservative values, were surprisingly supportive of their daughter's acting out. In an article archived by the website *LittleWillow.com*, her father John offered, "Maureen is a sensible girl and will be able to look after herself. I cannot see her getting into any kind of trouble."

By the time Maureen turned 14, she was looking for a way out. The convent curriculum was pointing her in the direction of what she perceived as a dreary future. She was of an age where getting out and about and having a good time was uppermost. So in what would be a bold move, Maureen left convent school, changed her birth name from Mary to Maureen and got what she perceived as a glamorous and hip job as a trainee manicurist/hairdresser at the Ashley Du Pre Salon. Maureen was still living at home but, in her mind, she was now on her own in a world that was electric with the onset of rock n' roll.

By age 15, Maureen had become a part of a new breed of rock groupies, young often aggressive girls who were regulars at places like The Cavern Club, a hot and sweaty Liverpool dive that, in those days, would feature the likes of Rory Storm and The Hurricanes and the up and coming new kids on the scene The Beatles. Shortly after joining this brave new rock n' roll world, Maureen had her first musician relationship, dating Rory Storm and The Hurricanes' guitarist Johnny Guitar for a brief period. But that experience would pale by comparison to the arrival of The Beatles on the scene which completely turned Maureen and the rest of the rock girls' heads around.

"They [the girls] used to hang around the Cavern Club, just on the off chance of seeing The Beatles coming or going," Maureen said in *The Beatles Bible* website. "They would come out of the lunchtime sessions [shows] and just stand outside all afternoon, queuing up for the evening shows."

Either by fear or guile, Maureen avoided that all day ritual. "I never joined the queue until two or three hours before the Cavern opened," she told *The Beatles Bible*. "What would be going on outside frightened me. There would always be fights and rows among the girls standing outside. When the doors opened the first girls would tear in, knocking each other over. When it got near the time when The Beatles would come on, the girls would go to the lavatory with their little carrying cases to get changed and made up so when The Beatles came on they'd look smashing as if they had just arrived."

The mania would often evolve into side bets among the girls on who could get The Beatles' attention. It was in those instances that Maureen would be particularly bold. In one instance she went up to Paul and kissed him. In a more telling situation she chanced upon Ringo in the street outside *The Cavern* and kissed him and got his autograph. True to be known, Maureen had a crush on Ringo, often citing his down to earth, laidback nature as a main attraction. Maureen would take every opportunity to be in Ringo's space but was, initially, not certain if he was interested in her. It would take three weeks but one night at The Cavern, Ringo asked her to dance. Maureen felt that he was interested but, initially, their romance was tentative.

"He asked to take me home," she related in an interview that appeared in *The London Evening Standard, Teen Life* and *Datebook*. "Okay I said but I have my girlfriend with me. He took us both home and for the next six weeks. The three of us were getting quite friendly. One day he said to me 'Could we go out one night? And could it be just you and me?' I said okay."

That first date was just a stroll around the Liverpool streets, walking and talking. They began seeing each other on a regular basis. To say that Maureen was bowled over to be with Ringo was an understatement as she enthused to *The Telegraph*. "Here I was a silly 16 year-old hairdresser and dating the most popular drummer in Liverpool." It was in those early days of their courtship that Maureen's feelings for the man she called Richy came into focus. "Richy is such a cheerful, peaceful man," she told *Le Chroniquer*. "He has a wonderful sense of humor and can be very charming."

But what Maureen would quickly discover was that her sudden status as Ringo's girlfriend made her a marked woman in her girl/groupie clique. "I had to be careful because of the fans. I might easily have been killed otherwise. None of them were supposed to have steady girlfriends," she told *thefabfour blog*. Maureen would do her best to be discreet but would constantly be the target of threats and harassment that would ultimately cause her to quit the only job she would ever have. On February 14, 1963, the threats would turn violent when, while waiting for the band outside the Locarno Ballroom, she was attacked by a jealous fan who clawed Maureen's face with her fingernails.

Maureen soon found some measure of employment when The Beatles, no doubt with a subtle push from Ringo, hired her to act in a managerial capacity for The Beatles growing fan club. For Maureen, it was not a taxing situation. She read fan letters and respond to them. But it did keep Ringo and Maureen together in some form.

With The Beatles growing in popularity, their relationship became a challenge and a long distance one at that. The band was now on the verge of stardom and that meant more time in London and seemingly always on tour. Maureen, who had by this time turned 17, was still living with her parents. The band did not have much time off, usually a Monday when the clubs were not booking and the couple took advantage of what little time together they could muster. Ringo would come up to Liverpool and they would play girlfriend/boyfriend in a time honored way. Going to a movie, a pup, a restaurant or a show.

By this time, Maureen had ingratiated herself into what was unofficially The Beatle Wives Club, a loose conglomeration of wives and girlfriends. In all honesty, The Beatles' worldview when it came to women was largely paternalistic. Music and their careers came first and their women came second. And it was a situation that the women in their lives went along with. A lot of time was spent waiting outside of clubs and halls for their men to finish for the night or waiting for a late recording session to end and they returned home. Which left a lot of time for Maureen and the others to enjoy the perks, endless shopping, eating at fine restaurants and getting together in 'hen sessions' to talk about their day and, just as often, the trials and tribulations of being with a Beatle. And in that setting, Maureen, despite being less worldly or accomplished than the other women, seemed to fit in quite well.

Like just about everything else surrounding her private life, Maureen was mum on how she got along with the other ladies but there were others who were around the scene who dropped bits and pieces of how Maureen fit in. Former Beatles Press Officer Tony Barrow pointed out in *Musicoholics.com* that "Maureen was a chirpy sort with a profane sense of humor." Long time scenester and Beatle insider Chris O'Dell also, in the same *Musicoholics.com* piece offered that "Maureen was the type of girl that got along with everyone. Despite the pressure of dating a Beatle, she was not afraid to be her own person."

Easily, her most important alliance among the other Beatle wives was Cynthia. They both came from the same general area and had a similar straightforward attitude about things. Cynthia would recount the chemistry between the two women during that period in an excerpt from *WithTheBeatleGirls.com*. "Far from being a shy little thing, Maureen was talkative, full of laughter and great fun. Maureen was one of the most down to earth, honest people I ever knew."

Especially when it pertained to being straightforward about the status of her relationship. Into 1963 it had all been a clandestine affair, not hiding from being with Ringo but, in terms of the prying eyes of the press, it was an unofficial secret that finally went public in 1963 when Maureen and Ringo accompanied McCartney and his girlfriend Jane Asher on a holiday in Greece. By this time The Beatles were big enough that the media was dogging them at every turn and, shortly after returning from Greece and turning 18, her normal aversion to doing interviews gave way to a not unusual bit of candor when asked by *The Daily Express* if Ringo and she were about to tie the knot.

"We are not getting married, that's for sure," she revealed. "I am a girlfriend and no more. It's just an ordinary girl/boy affair. There is nothing serious about it."

But, years later, Maureen would acknowledge in a rare interview with *Le Chroniqueur* that the Greece holiday would also give her a heretofore different look at Ringo. "I was finding that he had this real big inferiority complex about him. He just constantly wanted me to reassure him that I loved him because he gets so afraid. We would be lying in bed and he would hold me close to him and say 'Do you really love me?' I would constantly have to reassure him that I did. He was just so afraid that I might not love him."

But by the following year, the relationship, at least from Maureen's perspective, would turn much more serious, occasioned by a frightening incident in which Ringo suddenly collapsed during a pre-tour photo session and was rushed to a nearby hospital where it was found that he had a bad case of tonsillitis and a fever of 103. Maureen immediately moved from her home in Liverpool to his flat in London. She visited Ringo daily during his eventual recovery, bringing him gifts and ice cream. Ringo was touched by Maureen's loyalty and love and once he was fully recovered, he proposed to her one night at *The Ad Lib Club*. Maureen immediately said yes.

The consensus was, even for those with a penchant for liking Maureen, that she was still the groupie who got lucky. Michael Seth Starr, author of the book *Ringo With a Little Help*, offered in a 2020 interview with the author that nothing could be further from the truth. "I don't agree with the assessment that Maureen was a groupie. Maureen was truly in love with Ringo, not for his status as a Beatle but for who he was as a person. Maureen and Ringo came from similar backgrounds in Liverpool and had a lot in common. I do believe the love between Ringo and Maureen was genuine."

But in typical 60's/Ringo/too many drinks fashion as Maureen would recall on her honeymoon during a gaggle of press interviews that was chronicled by *The BeatleUltimate Experience.com*. "I could tell that Ringo was sort of thinking about it and just sort of said 'Will you marry me?' And I said 'Yes... Have another drink.' And we did [have another drink] and that was it."

Of course this being in the middle of the first wave of Beatlemania, a ring and a date would take some scheduling. But in early January 1964, nature would take its course when Maureen discovered that she was pregnant. Maureen was happy to discover that Ringo was thrilled at the news and the wheels were quickly set in motion for a quickie, low-key marriage headed up by manager Epstein who, after a similar situation with John and Cynthia, had become quite the expert at such matters. But with the Beatles now constantly under the press scrutiny, the notion of low-key and intimate immediately went out the window.

Lennon, Harrison and a small circle of family and friends were reportedly joined by an estimated 100 journalists and photographers, which succeeded in turning what should have been a simple civil ceremony at the Caxton-Hall Registrars Office in London on February 11, 1965 into a bit of a sideshow. But by that time, Maureen appeared to have a handle on what it took to be a Beatle wife. She smiled a lot, said little when talked to and basically faded into the background as the most important day in her life unfolded. Maureen had been in on The Beatles rise to stardom, she had witnessed and, yes, been a part of the craziness that had grown in a short period of time. By the time, Ringo and she had said their 'I do's, Maureen was ready to take the long ride on the back of worldwide celebrity and into obscurity.

She recalled in a *LittleWillows.com* story that she had become the perfect Beatle wife by learning to hide in the background. "I might have been killed otherwise. The other girls were not friendly at all once they heard the news. They wanted to stab me in the back."

Maureen's on the job training would continue during a three-day holiday in Sussex. Hoping for a few days of privacy and bliss before Ringo had to go back to work, the couple was sadly surprised when word had been leaked to the press and after their first night together, they awoke to literally dozens of reporters and photographers snapping pictures and firing questions. They were both annoyed at the intrusion on their privacy but consented to a couple of brief interviews in which Ringo did most of the talking while Maureen responded with the likes of "Yes, yes" and 'No, it's great." When asked how she felt about the fact that she could not go anywhere with her husband without being mobbed, Maureen essentially laid out her blueprint for her future when she said, "I don't worry about it. I just sort of enjoy myself."

Very early in their relationship, Ringo had offered to set Maureen up with a national chain of hairdressing salons. But when the hectic life of being a Beatle and, in the case of Maureen, of being a Beatle wife and mother kept getting in the way, the promise would eventually fade away with nary a protest from Maureen. Because truth be told, she was, well into her pregnancy, quite content to sit back and be the model wife and mother.

And the reality is that Maureen now officially had the ideal life. She was good friends with fellow wives Pattie and Cynthia with whom she would often spend many days shopping and just being a Beatle wife. Money was no object and, according to a report in *The Daily Mirror*, Ringo, or rather the financial bean counters of the growing Beatles empire, would give Maureen however much she needed 'as and when it was needed.' In the same article, Maureen acknowledged that she had no knowledge of money, taxation or life and, yes, she was living quite the lavish lifestyle. She would describe herself as "being as thick as two short planks" when it came to real world issues. But on September 13, 1965, the only real world issue that mattered was the birth of Ringo and Maureen's first child, Zak Starkey.

Since her marriage and the birth of their son, the at large impression of Maureen from the outside world seemed to soften. Oh, there were a few hangers on from her groupie days who still held a grudge against Maureen for having captured the prize. But, to a very large extent, Maureen was now the belle of the pop ball. Maureen was suddenly being inundated with offers to model maternity wear and preside over church bazaars, estate sales and was even mentioned in a very serious campaign to make her Mother of the Year but Maureen would, politely, turn all the invitations and opportunities down. To her way of thinking marriage and motherhood was the perfect opportunity to fade even further into the background.

To the surprise of many who still remembered Maureen from her 'wild child' days, the new wife and mother had evolved quite naturally into a very efficient and competent housewife. "I'm finding married life wonderful," she said in *TruthAboutTheBeatleGirls.com*. "I'm in the kitchen as much as possible, fiddling about and experimenting."

Author Starr indicated to this author that she may well have been happy with her situation but, in hindsight, she may well have fallen in line with the Beatles' blueprint. "Maureen did follow the rules laid down by Brian Epstein regarding Beatle Wives. She kept an extremely low profile, gave few interviews, all in order to keep up the appearance of Ringo being 'available' to adoring female fans. That was, in retrospect, an insulting and emotionally humiliating way to be treated. But Maureen followed the rules and did as instructed which could not have been easy for her."

Maureen had grown to deal with the reality of her husband being on the road or in the studio so often by being on the phone daily with old and new friends, occasionally meeting up with old girlfriends from back in the day for a snack and a chat and putting her haircutting skills to good use by going over to Ringo's parents house to give them a touch up. But all those diversions aside, her main chore was Zak 24/7 and, coming in a close second, the care and feeding of her husband. By necessity, Maureen had grown to be an early riser and so it was not uncommon when Ringo would come home, often as late or early as 4:00 a.m., he would find Maureen already up, handing him a cup of tea and going about making his breakfast.

On the surface, the marriage of Maureen and Ringo seemed the most stable of all the Beatle relationships. Two more children, Jason Starkey born August 19, 1967 and Lee Starkey born November 11, 1970, were testament to the strength and commitment of the couple. And it would go without saying that Maureen would turn out to be the most forgiving wife on the planet. The temptations of stardom were not lost on Ringo and, over the course of their marriage, there were consistent reports of infidelities and frequent drunken episodes. By this time, Maureen was well aware of the realities of life on the road and, to the world at large, it seemed that there was an understanding between the couple. Ringo would always return to her, apologetic, and Maureen would take him back.

Author Michael Seth Starr pointed to the difference between Maureen and Ringo's relationship and those of the other Beatles. "While the stories of John, Paul and George's womanizing as Beatles are legion, you rarely, if ever, heard or read anything about Ringo's extramarital escapades during his time with the Beatles and that says a lot."

With the success and relative stability of the Beatles' relationships, the group had begun to change in regards to the presence of their women in their working lives. Some speculate that John allowing Yoko to show up at recording sessions had opened the floodgates to the rest of the wives and serious girlfriends coming along. In any case, by the time sessions for what would become the *White Album* were underway, Maureen recalled in *Le Chroniquer* that Ringo extended an invitation.

"I went to a couple of studio sessions. It was only because he asked me, not because I wanted to. I was so used to him coming home from the studio and me sitting up 'til the crack of dawn waiting for him, that going to his work would be so out of the ordinary. So I told him that if he wanted me to go that I would."

Maureen had to admit that watching the Beatles at work was an eye opening experience after so many years of being largely kept in the dark about what transpired in the studio. In conversation with *Le Chroniquer*, she likened the experience to watching actors sparring over lines. "I would sit there with a cup of coffee in my hand or gossip with the other Beatle wives. When I did watch them, I always thought to myself 'So this is what Ringo has been doing for the last six years. I sometimes felt like a fly on the wall. But I knew I had to be the luckiest fly in the world."

Maureen was also in the often uncomfortable position of witnessing the demise of The Beatles. The reasons were numerous and often a mixture of many. Financial. The pressures of stardom and touring. Yoko Ono's presence both personally and professionally. Creative differences. All of which had combined to drive a wedge between the long time friends, a wedge that no amount of money and potential could heal. And it was Maureen who was home the day Ringo stormed in and announced that, after yet another row with Paul, he was quitting the band.

"I was surprised when he came home so soon," she recalled in *Le Chroniquer*. "He told me to pack my bags without giving me much of an explanation. But I could see the distress in his eyes. It was just painful. I fought with him for a while and told him it was foolish to go away so soon. But I could tell that he really didn't care at that point."

The Beatles would officially call it quits in 1968 with one last performance on the rooftop of the Apple Records building. As the concert wound down, video and audio would record that Paul would turn in the direction of Maureen and shout out "Thanks Mo."

Although they made a pretense of staying in touch for a time, inevitably the members of The Beatles and their families soon went their separate ways. Maureen recalled the depression that inevitably enveloped her husband and drove him deep into the throes of alcoholism. "His inferiority complex, his low self esteem," she reflected in *Le Chroniquer*. "In a way I think that's why he turned to drinking so heavily. I think he used it as a cloth to hide his perceived weaknesses and failures. He would drink to get plastered to hide from it but he knew that, eventually, he couldn't hide."

During one particularly dark moment, Maureen reported to *Le Chroniquer* that she came upon Ringo attempting to commit suicide. "He tried to cut his throat with a razor in the bathroom. I don't think it took place when he was drunk (or at least I don't think so). He really frightened me. But I knew he wasn't conscious of what he was trying to do. It was something he wouldn't have done if he was conscious."

Author Michael Seth Starr told the author that he felt the end of The Beatles pretty much sealed the end of Maureen and Ringo's marriage and that a lot of the burden had fallen on Maureen who was attempting to raise three children while dealing with a husband who was drowning himself in drink and depression. "I think by that point in her marriage to Ringo, Maureen was at the end of her rope emotionally and that she and Ringo had grown apart. They were victims of the in fighting among the Beatles that led to the band's breakup. It was a very unhappy time for everyone involved and I suppose Maureen was feeling particularly vulnerable and ignored."

Which would make Maureen susceptible to the not too veiled seduction at the hands of one of Ringo's closest friends, George Harrison. By 1970, Harrison and his wife Pattie had reconnected with Ringo and Maureen and would occasionally get together for small intimate dinners at each other's homes. Initially the vibe at these visits was laidback and convivial. But, as chronicled in the book *Behind Sad Eyes: The Life of George Harrison*, Pattie would soon notice that her husband was taking more than a friendly interest in Maureen.

One night Ringo and Maureen invited George and Pattie to their house for dinner. After dinner, and in a mellow mood, George picked up a guitar and began playing a series of love songs. Suddenly he stopped playing, looked at Maureen who was sitting next to Ringo and said, "I'm in love with you Maureen." Maureen was visibly upset. Ringo raged at George and then stormed out of the room. Pattie, totally mortified, burst into tears and locked herself in Ringo's bathroom. What Maureen was feeling at that point was anybody's guess.

A few weeks after the incident, Pattie returned home from shopping to find Maureen and George in bed together. Pattie would not need any more proof that something was going on. But, as she explained in an interview with *StartsAt60.com*, "I became truly aware that there was an affair going on when she [Maureen] would turn up at our house around midnight and she would still be there the next day. I'd have to be pretty stupid not to notice."

In a fit of total revenge, Pattie called Ringo and told him exactly what was going on between her husband and his wife. "Obviously Ringo was seriously pissed off," Pattie reflected in a *Goldmine* interview. "But I don't know whether his anger was directed more to Maureen or George."

Ringo immediately threatened divorce. How long the affair between

Maureen and George went on is undetermined. But with the specter of divorce looming over her head, Maureen, in what many perceived as a last ditch attempt to save their marriage, floated her version of the affair with George as something that was never sexual in nature and that she was still in love with Ringo and wanted to stay with him.

All of which would put Pattie in an uncomfortable situation when, through social and Beatle related events, she would come in contact with Maureen. In a 106.3 The Fox radio interview some years later, Pattie acknowledged that she had taken the high road when Maureen and she would meet. "I would be civil to her afterwards. I could forgive but I couldn't forget. She [Maureen] always seemed to be really angry with George. I think she thought that they would stay together. I don't know what her desire was. I didn't know what she was hoping for. Maybe she thought that she would be with George and she found out that he didn't want that."

Ringo's divorce proceedings were stopped and the couple continued to live together in an uneasy climate, for the sake of the kids, but the relationship did not seem to rebound. To what degree Maureen remained faithful after George is open to conjecture but what was certain was that Ringo's drinking became an even bigger issue and his own infidelities became even more blatant. Most notably, while still married to Maureen, Ringo began flaunting a very public affair with model Nancy Lee Andrews.

Finally Maureen had enough and filed for divorce on the grounds of Ringo's infidelity, although there would be suggestions that Ringo's alcoholism, reported emotional abuse and being an absent father most certainly weighed into the equation. Maureen admitted that she knew nothing about the machinations of the legal process and so endured many months of litigation, arguments over financial support and child visitation for Ringo and the continuing questions about her financial settlement and the seemingly lack of talent, according to Maureen, on the part of her lawyers.

Throw in the fact that, through it all she was still in love with Ringo, and Maureen was emotionally and psychologically at her wits end by the time the divorce was finalized on July 17, 1975. She realized that she had never really been out in the world and had few survival skills and was suddenly scared to death at the prospect of having to live the rest of her life on her own.

And in her lowest moments during that first post divorce year, Maureen attempted suicide by riding a motorbike into a brick wall. The attempt resulted in Maureen sustaining severe facial damage and required extensive surgery to repair her face. In a bit of an about face, Maureen's attempt at taking her own life succeeded in turning her life around. Mentally and emotionally, she rebounded and was seemingly up to dealing with life without the shadows of Ringo and The Beatles following her.

In short order she was dating Hard Rock Café co-founder Isaac Tigrett, a man of means and charisma. Sparks immediately flew between the couple and, into 1976, they would be living together in bliss. That Maureen was so deeply involved after a short period after leaving Ringo had many speculating on a number of levels. It might well be the classic rebound relationship. Or it could have been a relationship of convenience for Maureen who had never been without a man of means who could shield her from the real world. Neither Maureen nor Tigrett had much to say on the subject. For his part, Tigrett, a big money spender when it came to pop culture memorabilia, once described his relationship with Maureen as being "his ultimate collectible." Maureen, who had not lost her street sense of humor over the years, would often describe her relationship with Tigrett this way "Just give me furs, jewels and property. Thank you."

Whatever the reason, the relationship seemed to work. The couple were together for a decade before Maureen gave birth to a baby girl, Augusta King Tigrett in 1987. Maureen and Tigrett would marry in 1990.

After Ringo, Maureen continued to live the life of relative luxury, security and, light years removed from the turmoil of the Beatlemania days, had found a degree of peace and contentment in her life. "I've lived through a lot and I've learned a lot," she said in the book *The Beatles: Here, There and Everywhere*. "I'd say I'm a happier person these days. I'm happy with my life now. I've learned to be content and I've matured."

On September 7, 1985, Maureen became a grandmother when her son Jason and his wife welcomed a baby daughter. Becoming grandparents seemed to rekindle a friendship between Maureen and Ringo, They had always remained amicable, largely due to their children, but now seemed more inclined to remember the good times. Maureen over the years would remain stalwart in acknowledging that she still loved her ex-husband.

On April 4, 1994, Maureen suddenly collapsed in Los Angeles while on a business trip with her husband. Initially doctors described the incident as being the result of her being anemic. Two weeks later, a further examination indicated that she, in fact, had leukemia. Maureen was flown to *The Fred Hutchinson Cancer Research Center* in Seattle, Washington in October of 1994. During her stay, Ringo would be a regular visitor to the hospital. Reportedly it was at Ringo's suggestion that his oldest son Zak, whose blood type closely matched his mother's, donated bone marrow, blood platelets and white blood cells, to his mother. Sadly, complications from the bone marrow transplant resulted in a fungal infection that by this time frail Maureen could not overcome.

Maureen slipped away on December 30, 1994 at the age of 48. Family and friends had gathered around her in her final moments. Tigrett held one hand while Ringo held the other. With tears streaming down his face, Ringo said, "I love you." Over and over as Maureen passed.

Chapter Three
Pattie Boyd Harrison/Clapton

Interviews and features about Pattie Boyd are consistent on a number of levels. They fairly quickly focus on the fact that, at one time, Pattie was married to both George Harrison and Eric Clapton and subsequently divorced from both. The irony in these pieces is that while both marriages ended, Pattie was in these legendary musician's lives to inspire some of the greatest rock music songs in history.

During her time with Harrison, Pattie was the inspiration/muse for the songs 'I Need You' (1965), 'Something' (1969), 'For You Blue (1970) and 'So Sad' (1974). Likewise, her time with Clapton inspired the guitar legend to pen the classic "Layla" (1970), "Wonderful Tonight" (1977) and "She's Waiting" (1985). Over the years, the image of muse has followed Pattie through countless stories and interviews. And in each case, she has taken the concept of being a muse of legendary proportions in a thoughtful, nonegotistical manner.

"You can't help but think that people will look at you and go 'Oh my God! What is it about her that is so special that a song is being written about her,'" she told *Goldmine*. "Maybe I never thought about the joys of it at the time because it was so beautiful and flattering to be in." In an interview with *Harper's Bazaar*, Pattie dug deeper into the concept when she offered. "I think, in both cases, George and Eric had an inability to communicate their feelings through normal conversation so, in that sense, I became a reflection for them."

Colin Ian Langdon Boyd and Diana Francis Drysdale married on September 14, 1942. The story was typical of life during wartime. They had met at a dance. He was a dashing Royal Air Force man and she was an attractive young woman enraptured with the idea of a wartime romance with a tall, handsome military man. He proposed after only a handful of dates before going off to battle, survived an injury and came back physically and emotionally scarred.

Everything about the relationship did not seem right and marriage, to all right-thinking people, seemed out of the question. Pattie said as much in a passage from her book *Wonderful Tonight.* "My parents married when they were young and inexperienced. They knew next to nothing about each other when they walked down the aisle."

Pattie would be much more candid in assessing her parent's courtship and marriage in an excerpt from a *Sydney Morning Herald* article. "My mother met my father at a dance at age 16. He was handsome, in the army and they fell in love. He became a pilot, had a bad crash and was hospitalized. He was badly damaged but my mother had promised to marry him. She felt she had to go through with the marriage."

Pattie Boyd was born on March 17, 1944. Like just about everything connected to her parent's life and relationship, her birth was typical of the dysfunction. Her parents were so convinced that the child would be a boy that they already had the name Michael picked out. Pattie would be almost an afterthought when they discovered their firstborn was a girl. "My father didn't even remember me being born," she said to the *Sydney Morning Herald*, "which seemed odd to me. He was very quiet. I never really knew if he loved me."

Due to his military obligations, the Boyd family was constantly on the move, living in Scotland, Surrey and Kenya. Along the way the couple had three more children which meant a full house that resulted in Pattie's parents becoming more distant and distracted when it came to giving Pattie the attention a young child needed. "I don't have any recollection of my father talking to me or communicating with me," Pattie told *The Guardian*. "He was very remote. I think the war had made him slightly damaged."

But she refused to simply blame her father for the coldness she experienced growing up as she explained in *South Coast Today* magazine. "My parents behaved in the way they'd been treated as children themselves, which was really austere, children were seen and not really spoken to. "

Pattie saw the family's time in Kenya in various shades of light and dark. They stayed with Diane's parents, an old school couple with a sense of decency and good humor about them. Life in Kenya was largely a time of childhood happiness and growing up in a fantasy. But there was also the reality of living with parents whose love for each other had long since passed and it would reflect in their day-to-day dealings with their children. "Colin [her younger brother] and I were both sent to Catholic boarding school when I was eight," she told *The Sydney Morning Herald*. "I remember begging my mother to let me stay home. I didn't understand why they didn't want me at home. I guess my mother had too many children and wanted to clear the deck a little."

Within the next year, Pattie and the rest of the Boyd children would experience further trauma. Pattie's father had become enamored of a neighbor woman and Pattie's parents would soon divorce. In short order, Diane would begin dating and quickly became engaged and married to Robert Garner Jones. "My mother moved to England with my stepfather and my two younger sisters and left Colin and I with our father in Kenya for a few months," said the excerpt in *The Sydney Morning Herald*. "I was scared and confused. I had no idea what was going on. Finally, she sent for my brother and I and we flew, separately, to England. It felt like a terrible dream when she introduced our stepfather to us and said 'Meet your new father.'"

Hoping for the best in her new life in England, Pattie, sadly, found just a variation on her old life. Her stepfather, Robert, had a bullying streak that would often manifest itself in various forms of physical and emotional abuse, much of it directed toward Pattie and her siblings. Pattie's mother, who by that time had given birth to another child with her second husband, was so emotionally and psychologically beaten down and submissive that she would never go to her children's defense. It was during what would become a seven-year odyssey of changing schools, changing homes and feeling a social and psychological outcast at every turn, that Pattie, just into her early teen years, was feeling much older and psychologically adrift. She would acknowledge as much in *Brainyquote.com* when she described herself as "During my childhood, I felt much older than my years because I always felt responsible for my brothers and sisters."

Which left little time for Pattie to just be a normal teenager. Her parents forbade Pattie to go to the movies alone or with someone they did not know or approve of. Her television viewing was closely monitored. And it went without saying that dating was out of the question.

"I didn't have boyfriends until my late teens," she recalled to *The Guardian*. "My stepfather disapproved of me going out with anybody. I never really came across any boys for quite a time. When I did and one of them asked me out, I was petrified." Pattie remembered her own personal right of passage, her first kiss with a boy, in a quote from *The Sydney Morning Herald*. "I had my first kiss around age 16 with a local boy who played tennis. That moment was exciting but, at that time, I viewed boys as brothers more than the kissing kind."

Pattie would make her way through three different schools by the time she turned 17. She had been good in some subjects and not so good in others but she managed to get the equivalent of high marks on the often bumpy road to ending her formal education. She still felt detached in terms of any future goals and would often acknowledge that the years of school had led her to nothing more than a future of marriage and children. To add even further stress to her family situation, her stepfather left Pattie's mother for another woman, leaving Diane a broken woman saddled with no money and, because of the two children she had with Robert, now saddled with six children and no future.

Pattie remembered those sad, confusing and bleak times in her book *Wonderful Tonight*. "In March 1961 I turned 17 at the end of the summer term and said farewell to school. My parents had never been particularly interested in my education, university had never been mentioned and I had no idea what I might do before I got married. My only ambition was to get away from the dysfunctional family we had become."

Pattie toyed with the idea of becoming an airline hostess, a secretary and even with the idea of becoming a violinist before her mother managed to use her meager connection in the beauty industry to get her daughter an apprentice shampooing job at a London beauty salon. Pattie was thrilled. She moved into a house with three other girls in South Kensington. From the outset Pattie experienced the bohemian life. She had little if any money and would once boast that she subsisted on frozen chicken pies. But being away from her family made it all worthwhile. "The sense of freedom was intoxicating," she recalled in her book *Wonderful Tonight*. "No more nuns, no more Bobbie [stepfather] and no more tension."

She would further enthuse about her newfound freedom in *South Coast Today*. "When the 60's emerged, there was suddenly all this freedom. It was like being able to be a child. It was really special.

Pattie thrived in this new, exciting and totally free environment that was the early 60's. Breakthroughs in music, fashion and lifestyles were on the march, driven to a large extent by the arrival of The Beatles. Pattie seemed to fit right in. "I was never a beauty, not in a classical sense, although I knew I was pretty," she self-assessed in *The Guardian*. It would be those qualities, combined with a sense of larger than life enthusiasm, that would make her the darling of customers in the salon, one in particular, who worked for the hip *Honey Magazine*, suggested that Pattie should get into modeling.

The concept of modeling was alien to Pattie. She knew the images of the beautiful people who leaped out of photo spreads and covers of magazines. But once she decided to give it a try, she quickly discovered how hard a hustle it really was.

Pattie would spend each day making the rounds of photographers, trying to persuade them to use her in their photo shoots and, early on, she faced often cruel rejection, being dismissed with such comments as she looked too much like a rabbit and being admonished for not knowing how to do her hair and makeup. And it was during these lean days that Pattie had her first brushes with the casting couch.

"Some photographers would try hitting on me," she reflected in the *Sydney Morning Herald*, "but I didn't submit and say 'Oh must I?' I would get out of there and then warn the other girls."

But not surprisingly, the person Pattie would consider her first serious boyfriend would turn out to be a photographer named Jean Claude. Pattie spoke fondly of him in the *Sydney Morning Herald*. "He was handsome and encouraged me to be a model. We only kissed and eventually he left me for another girl. But we remained friends."

Eventually Pattie's struggles were rewarded with the changing times. Slickness and sophistication were suddenly a thing of the past. In its place was a newfound sense of 60's look and style that was taking its cue from the rise of modern music and lifestyle expression. Once considered a rabbit, Pattie was now considered what was becoming the hip style in fashion. "I did well because my image was slightly different," she explained to *The Guardian*. "I looked younger than previous models. I had the long blonde hair and big, innocent eyes." It also did not hurt Pattie's career hopes that she had long legs and looked fetching in a mini skirt. Pattie's career began to take off. She landed an agent and would embark on a two year odyssey that would see her become the 'it' girl of modern 60's fashion.

Pattie began to model extensively in London and Paris. She would marvel that she had suddenly become the toast of the fashion world. "I was a model working with some of the most successful photographers in

London, people like David Bailey, Terence Donovan and Brian Duffy," she told *The Daily Mail*. "I was appearing in newspapers and magazines like *Vanity Fair* and *Vogue*."

She would later offer in a *Huffington Post* interview that being a model seemed a perfect fit for her shy and retiring nature. "I liked being a model because you didn't have to say anything. You just had to stand there and pose. You could hide behind the makeup and clothes."

By late 1963, Pattie was once again involved in what she considered her first real relationship with another photographer named Eric Swayne. Love, or what seemed to pass for love in the swinging 60's, was all part of a suddenly exciting ride. Swayne was serious to a degree but not all that serious. But she would later concede that she liked the closeness of being in a relationship.

Nineteen sixty-four would see her move up the modeling hierarchy to do television commercials, first for a car wash shampoo called *DOP*, then for a snack food called *Smith's Crisps* which was directed by then up-and-coming director Richard Lester. Pattie didn't think a whole lot about the acting process, especially when, in 1964, she got an uncredited part as the Girl in the Restaurant in a comedic romp called *Nothing But The Best* which, she determined, was far less glamorous than being a model.

"My agent called me one day to tell me that there was a casting audition to go to," she related in a *Goldmine* interview. "When I arrived for the audition I recognized the director [Lester] because I had done some television commercials with him. I did the audition and then went home. The next thing I knew, I had gotten a phone call from my agent with the news that I had gotten a part in a Beatles film called *A Hard Days Night*. I was a bit stunned by this. I never really had the desire or ambition to be an actress. But my agent said, 'Oh don't worry. It's just a walk on part,' in which Pattie would play a bit as a school girl with a one word line of dialogue 'Prisoners.'

On the day of the shoot. Pattie took a train to the Paddington Station, just outside of London, where the train stopped. Pattie and the other girls immediately spotted The Beatles on the platform. They boarded the train and introduced themselves to the girls before going off to film. Pattie recalled in *Goldmine* that The Beatles were "so charming" but that she immediately set her eyes on Harrison. "He was so unbelievably good looking and adorable. In a sense George and I just hit it off."

During a lunch break that day Pattie and George sat together. "I remember feeling so silly because I was still dressed in a stupid schoolgirl uniform," she said to *Goldmine*. "We were both really shy but we enjoyed sitting next to each other and talking a bit. Being close to him was electrifying."

At the end of the day's shoot, the train was heading back to London when Harrison made his move as Pattie recalled in *Goldmine*. "George looked at me and said 'Will you marry me?' I just laughed as if he were joking. Then he said 'Can I take you out to dinner tonight?' Then I said 'Well, actually, I'm going out with my boyfriend but you can come along too.' He said 'No, he said that wasn't the idea at all.'"

There would be a few days break before Pattie returned to the set of *A Hard Days Night*. Which would give her time to make an important personal and emotional decision. She and Eric Swayne had been a couple for two years and Swayne had spoken often about marriage. But there had been something about meeting Harrison that had hit a nerve. It was love at first sight. And so Pattie took the days off to break up with Swayne who reportedly did not take it well. Pattie was now free to follow her heart. Upon returning to the set of *A Hard Days Night*, Harrison once again asked her out. This time she accepted.

Their first date was at the prestigious *Garrick Club*. The young couple were, as was often the case when members of The Beatles were out socially, chaperoned by Brian Epstein. Epstein was an old hand at such situations at this point, a good conversationalist and a bit of a buffer in this case as both Pattie and Harrison were a bit nervous as Pattie would admit in her book *Wonderful Tonight*. "If George and I, two young shy people, had been on our own in such a grown up restaurant, it would have been too intense. As it was, we had a lovely evening, sitting side by side, hardly daring to touch each other's hand."

Their mutual attraction was palpable and, within a matter of weeks, they were a couple. "I thought he was absolutely adorable," Pattie gushed in an interview with *ABC News*. "He was very terribly good looking but really funny as well and just enchanting."

Pattie had never seen The Beatles perform live but, a few months after she and Harrison began dating, she would get the opportunity when, in 1964, The Beatles played a concert at the famed Hammersmith Odeon. Pattie recalled in an interview with *Goldmine* that the experience had been a bit of culture shock. "I was given a seat right near the front. The audience was screaming all of the time. To me, that was odd because I didn't realize that was what happened during their shows. The noise was huge."

As their relationship flourished, Pattie would begin to experience what it was like being the girlfriend of a Beatle during the height of Beatlemania. It was a time of excitement and experimentation in which young, hip creative people were setting the trends and styles. At the vanguard of this cultural revolution was the music and The Beatles. Pattie would reap the benefits of already being an accomplished model as well as the better half of Harrison. Her modeling assignments suddenly became more prestigious and high profile. As the new face of the moment, Pattie was approached at every turn with opportunity. She was recruited by a high profile teen magazine to pen a monthly frothy gossip and fashion column.

But there was a downside to the notoriety. Pattie and Harrison were both quite busy at their respective careers and, as Pattie offered in *South Coast Today*, it often made their relationship difficult. "I was working modeling and George would have to go off on tour every so often. What would be annoying for us is if the two things clashed."

Pattie, who had over the years cultivated a sense of gentility about her life, would find adjusting to the more aggressive side of Beatlemania a shock to her system. Once Harrison and she had become an item, she, as well as Harrison, would often find themselves in the crosshairs of aggressive fans. On the rare occasion when the couple would attempt to get away from the pressures of stardom for some quiet time alone, they would have to resort to disguises and false names when checking in and out of secluded getaways. Pattie's fake name of the day was often Miss Bond and she would regularly resort to wearing a black wig to throw off fans and media types alike.

But as Pattie would relate in *Harper's Bazaar* and *TheMorton Report.com* even the most elaborate dodges could not keep from putting her in some semblance of danger. "Sometimes, it was absolutely terrifying. One night I got to see The Beatles play at a theater in London and George told me that I should leave with my friends before the last number. So before the last song, we got up from our seats and walked toward the nearest exit door and there were these girls following behind us. They followed us out and they were kicking me and pulling my hair and pushing me all the way out the door. They were running after me.

One of my friends tried to hold them back and he said 'Just run to the car.' So me and the other girls ran to the car and just managed to get in and all these girls were rocking the car, trying to stop us from driving off. It was kind of scary."

It would be the constant intrusion of fans that forced Harrison to give up his London flat for a house in Surrey. Pattie moved in with him. Pattie relished the fantasy and dreamlike quality of those early days with Harrison which she shared in conversation with the *New Zealand Herald*. "Days would be so heady. We never had a weekend. It was all just wonderful days. Days and nights went into each other. Everyday was fabulous."

Pattie related in the *Sydney Morning Herald* that their relationship, spiritually, emotionally and romantically, was moving at a lightning speed. "We connected in every way and it [the relationship] was on very quickly. He was the one who wanted to get married. I was a bit cautious. My memories of marriage were of my mother having two husbands. Once George and I married, I didn't want to get divorced."

But Harrison would eventually wear Pattie's resistance down and he would once again pop the question in December 1965 in what Pattie would acknowledge in an *ABC News* interview was a very unromantic way, not atypical of how things were handled in the world of The Beatles. "One day he [George] said 'I really think we should get married. I'm going to go and speak to Brian about it.' After a bit, he came back, gave me a big kiss and said 'Brian said we can get married in January.'"

As with previous Beatle marriages, Epstein had it down to a very mechanical science. The marriage would be a low-key affair, taking place in a local registrar's office in Surrey on January 21, 1966. Epstein would once again serve as best man at a small gathering of family and friends, with McCartney being the only Beatle in attendance. All of which was done according to a template that would keep publicity to a minimum and thus not alienate the all-important female members of Beatles fandom.

"It was not the most glamorous place," Pattie recalled in her memoir *Wonderful Tonight*. "It was not the wedding I had dreamed of. I would have loved to have been married in a church but Brian didn't want a big fuss. They [The Beatles] all trusted him so implicitly that when he said it should be a quiet register office wedding, George agreed. He also said it had to be secret and if the press found out, it would be chaotic."

Despite Epstein's best efforts, or perhaps because of them, the happy couple had barely said their I do's when they were hit with a literal media onslaught as Pattie recalled in an *ABC News* conversation. "There was no shortage of pictures of us leaving the registrar's office. We came out into the street to find dozens of press photographers lined up outside. So much for keeping the whole thing secret."

With the cat out of the bag, Epstein, who knew the value of any kind of press surrounding The Beatles, called a hastily convened press conference the next day. The day after Pattie's special day was yet another three ring circus of inane and obvious softball questions aimed at the happy couple. "After the wedding, we had to endure a press conference," Pattie related in her book *Wonderful Tonight*. "It was so terrifying that I have almost blanked it from my memory. Just about the only thing that I remember is that I blurted out that we'd like three children but not immediately."

Owing to the never-ending Beatle business, Pattie and Harrison would not get off on their honeymoon in Barbados until early February. The days spent in Barbados proved to be some of Pattie's most memorable, frolicking in the sand and surf, having quiet, intimate dinners and basking in the bliss and glow of being newlyweds in love. "I was so happy I thought I might burst," she beamed in *Wonderful Tonight*. "It was bliss to have George all to myself, no work pulling either of us and no fans making life a misery."

The couple returned from their honeymoon and settled into their home in Surrey. Pattie had now found herself in a dream marriage and was willing to forego anything but hearth, home and making her man happy. When Harrison told Pattie that he would like her to stop working and to, essentially, become a housewife and, down the road, a mother, Pattie did not think twice about giving up a lucrative and satisfying career to become Mrs. George Harrison and embrace all the traditional values that went with it. And in conversation with *TheMortonReport.com*, she would made a strong case for that decision to, like Beatle wives had all done, fade into the background.

"It didn't occur to me that I had any creativity. I wasn't ambitious and so I really didn't think about myself in any way that wouldn't involve my husband. I sort of lived and partied and whatever and made my husband's life really happy and comfortable and enjoyable and warm and nurturing. And so I would do the whole traditional thing of looking after my man."

But while Pattie was more than familiar with all the insanity and fan frenzy that went with Beatlemania, she had, perhaps naively, felt that the mania would be tamped down once they had become husband and wife. But she recalled in *Goldmine* that once they returned home to Surrey, she discovered that nothing had changed.

"Obviously their fans followed them [The Beatles] everywhere they went. Before we had a gate put up outside of our house in Surrey, fans would come to our house all the time. On a couple of occasions some of my things were stolen. Depending on George's mood, more often than not, if fans came to the door, he would shoo them away. But if he was in a good mood, and they were nice people, he would be charming, sign autographs and have a few words with them. But it was an intrusion."

Those intrusions aside, Pattie soon found life married to a Beatle a dream come true. Harrison was often effusive in his love for Pattie, such as the time he told the *London Evening Standard,* "I married her because I loved her. We're a match for each other. She's my best friend." Pattie was likewise aware of the fantasy life she had bought into when she told *TheMortonReport.com* that, "It [her new life] was very normal to me. It was fantastic and I absolutely knew it. I was aware of how great it was and how fantastic it was. I knew this was absolutely the best and that it was joyous."

But the starry-eyed impressions aside, once married life settled into a semblance of normalcy, Pattie had occasion to examine her life in greater depth and realized that life among the beautiful people and the privileges afforded to being married to a rock star carried with it an emotional price. "Being with a celebrity can be so demeaning," she confessed to *TheMortonReport.com*. "And the thing is that once you've made your bed, you've got to lie in it. And so I created this nice cozy home and I couldn't get out of that mindset, being that person to try and strike an independent stance."

Nevertheless, Pattie would seemingly thrive early on in her marriage to Harrison as she recalled in *Startsat60.com*. "It was really fabulous in the beginning. We were both so young. We were able to go out, hang out and play. We had a wonderful time. He'd go off on tour and I'd hang out with my friends while we all waited for George to come back. It was very loving in the first few years"

But by the late 60's, Pattie and Harrison's relationship began to unravel, thanks, in large part, to the fact that the friendship between The

Beatles was becoming more and more antagonistic as the result of professional, creative and business differences bubbling to the surface. Harrison, in particular, had grown tired of the whole pop star thing and, emotionally, had withdrawn into a shell. Despite a growing interest in Indian mysticism and music, Harrison was drinking more and taking more drugs. And then there were the numerous infidelities which Pattie tolerated as being purely physical. She was philosophical about her husband's growing reputation as a serial philanderer and even admitted that part of the problem was hers in separate conversations with *The Guardian* and *The Sydney Morning Herald.*

"He was famous, good looking, had tons of money and flash cars. Girls were offering themselves everywhere and he loved it. To come home to old wifey must have been a bit dull. It's very seductive and easy to misbehave. Am I as much to blame? Probably because I didn't put my foot down. I didn't feel that I had the right to."

Adding to the growing problems in their marriage was the fact that Pattie and Harrison had remained childless. When the press began sniffing around that fact, Harrison, in perhaps his defining moments as Pattie's husband, would go public with the fact that the couple's inability to have children was his fault rather than Pattie's. Years later, Pattie would address the quite personal issue with *Mail Online.* "I thought that, naturally, when I grew up and got married I'd have children. Sadly, it didn't happen for me. I thought it just goes with the idea of being a woman. Then when it didn't happen, I started to panic and wondered why."

Harrison and Pattie would finally concede that they were not going to conceive a child on their own. Adoption was discussed and quickly dismissed by Harrison. The couples' marriage continued to disintegrate. Pattie began to notice that Harrison, emotionally, began to withdraw from her in a rigid way that highlighted his growing adherence to his interest in Indian religion and mysticism. She tried to articulate it in separate interviews with *Goldmine* and *Startat60.com*, "George and I just grew apart. He was angry a lot. We didn't talk much because all he was doing was chanting. The spell began to crumble. He didn't really confide in me. He was just so angry and he would just keep it all in. He didn't want to talk about anything."

As their marriage declined, Eric Clapton began to make his presence felt. Harrison and Clapton had gotten friendly in 1964 and had begun performing and recording together. Their relationship evolved into a deep-rooted friendship. Consequently, Clapton was always around and a growing infatuation with Pattie was brewing.

Around 1968, Pattie received an anonymous love letter from someone who had signed the letter with a cryptic E. It had not been the first time Pattie had received such a letter. Being a celebrity in her own rite and a Beatle wife to boot, such letters were common. Pattie showed the letter to Harrison who didn't think much of it. Shortly after receiving the letter, Clapton called Pattie up and asked if she had received his message. Pattie was confused and a bit frightened by Clapton's directness. Despite a marriage in tatters, Pattie still loved her husband. But she had to admit that she was intrigued.

Clapton's entry into Pattie's life would be the latest element of an already out of control period that would essentially last from 1969 to 1973. Harrison's affair with Ringo's wife some years into the 70's would only be the last straw of a doomed marriage. According to an observation by the late Delaney Bramlett who had invited Harrison on his Delaney, Bonnie and Friends tour in 1969 in the book *Behind Sad Eyes: The Life of George Harrison*, "There were thousands of groupies waiting for us to get back on the bus. He could have gotten sex if he wanted to. He was clearly in love with Pattie. I don't think he had any desire to cheat on her."

Bramlett's quote aside, there was much in Pattie's life that was restrictive.

Harrison's immersion in Indian religion did not allow for sex for pleasure. Harrison would continue to not allow Pattie to work. The ongoing question of the couple's inability to have children would continue to be a flashpoint in the marriage. Pattie took fertility tests that indicated there was nothing keeping the couple from conceiving which, rather than a positive, would result in several arguments and accusations. Nineteen sixty-nine would also mark the moment when the London police raided the couple's latest residence in Friar Park and arrested Pattie and Harrison on marijuana possession charges. On the surface, what should have been a minor news story was fueled by their celebrity into a front-page international story.

Pattie acknowledged in excerpts from *The Daily Mail* and her memoir *Wonderful Tonight* that those years were a nightmare. "That whole period was insane. We were all as drunk, stoned and single-minded as each other. Those last years of marriage were fueled by alcohol and cocaine. The drugs froze George's emotions and hardened his heart."

In the meantime, Clapton would continue to pursue Pattie. Hopping from the demise of Cream, the short-lived Blind Faith and the ambitious Derrick and The Dominos project, while slowly but surely descending into drug addiction, Pattie had become a fevered obsession of his. "I'd set myself up to fail," Clapton would recall in *Behind Sad Eyes: The Life of George Harrison.* "It was an impossible situation. It was an impossible situation for Pattie to cope with and for me to cope with."

Pattie, who by this time was emotionally all over the place as she attempted to hang onto her marriage, was upset by Clapton's antics as she revealed in *Behind Sad Eyes: The Life of George Harrison.* "I couldn't believe the situation that Eric had put me in. I thought it wasn't right and I thought our friendship was destined to end."

But the tension between Pattie and Harrison only served to increase the tension between Pattie and Clapton. "Eric had been making his desire for me clear for months," Pattie related in a *DailyMail.com* story. "I felt uncomfortable that he was pushing me in a direction in which I wasn't certain that I wanted to go."

The emotional tug of war would continue. Clapton persisted in expressing his desire for Pattie while the decline of love between Pattie and Harrison continued. One night in 1970, Pattie gave in.

As chronicled in *Behind Sad Eyes: The Life of George Harriso*n, there were two long reported and divergent versions of what happened. In the first, Harrison declined to accompany Pattie to a theater production of *Oh!Calcutta!* because he was hard at work on the album *All Things Must Come to Pass* and didn't blink an eye when Clapton offered to escort Pattie to the play. The more plausible story had Pattie attending the play alone and that Clapton showed up and sat down in the empty seat next to her. "After the interval at *Oh!Calcutta!* I came back to find Eric in the next seat. Afterward, we went to an after-party separately but ended up together," she was quoted in a *Daily Mail* story.

She was suddenly comfortable and feeling adventurous in Clapton's presence and when he suggested that Pattie might like to come back to his place and listen to a new song he had written, she threw caution to the wind and said yes. In a series of quotes that would appear in an extensive piece in the *Daily Mail*, Pattie disclosed what happened next.

"We went to his place. He switched on the tape machine, turned up the volume and played me the most powerful, moving song I had ever heard. It was "Layla," the story of a man who falls hopelessly in love with a woman who loves him but is unavailable. He played it for me two or three times, all the while watching my face intently for my reaction. My first thought was 'Oh God, everyone's going to know that this is about me.' But the realization that I had inspired such passion and creativity got the better of me. I could resist no longer."

Pattie and Clapton made wild, passionate love. Flushed with the emotion of the moment, they would return to the party they had been at. Only to discover that Harrison had apparently finished his work and had decided to meet up with his wife at the party. He spotted Pattie and Clapton walking hand and hand and looking very much in the romantic moment. In the book *Behind Sad Eyes: The Life of George Harrison*, it was chronicled that Harrison confronted the couple in what for Harrison was a totally irrational and jealous rage. He screamed at Clapton, warning him to never see his wife again. Clapton shot back with "I'm in love with your wife." Pattie was stunned and mortified as the two former friends raged at each other. Harrison turned on his wife, shoved her into his car and drove away.

This betrayal by Pattie and Clapton would seem to spell the end of the marriage or, at the very least, a trial separation. And for the first few days, tensions in the house were at a destructive level. But then, amazingly, things seemed to return to normal. Harrison had chosen to forgive and forget, to his way of thinking essentially putting the entire incident out of his mind. For her part, Pattie was at her wits end, her emotions running wild with thoughts of her continued love for Harrison and what she had shared with Clapton. For the better part of the following year, Pattie would regularly go off to be with Clapton. Which put her in a rather tenuous position when Harrison began his very public and upfront affair with Maureen around the same time.

Pattie's continued emotional and mental turmoil continued on a seemingly endless downward spiral. A very psychological connection emerged between Harrison and Pattie. She became increasingly withdrawn and largely reclusive. Which, as she explained in the *Daily Mail*, she had begun to consider ending it all. "My moods started to mirror George's and at times I felt almost suicidal. I don't think I was ever in any real danger of killing myself but I got as far as working out how I would do it. I would put on a diaphanous dress and throw myself off Beachy Head [a cliff]."

Not unlike her peers of the period, Pattie had dabbled in alcohol and drugs. But she pointed with pride to the fact that she knew when to stop. She would discover very early in her relationship with Clapton what not stopping would do to a person as she offered in terrifying detail in her book *Wonderful Tonight*.

"One day Eric showed up at our home. He showed me this packet of heroin and said 'Either you come away with me or I will take this.' I was appalled. I grabbed at it and tried to throw it away but he snatched it back. I turned him down and, for the next four years, he became a drug addict. At first I felt guilt. Then I felt anger because it was totally irrational of him to blame me for something he was probably going to do anyway. It was very selfish and destructive."

Without Clapton in her life, Pattie's life with Harrison had disintegrated into limbo. Both went through the motions of being husband and wife but the marriage was now a hollow shell. Pattie began to show signs of independence. Against Harrison's wishes, Pattie once again returned to modeling. When they were out and about socially it was more to keep up an illusion that was no longer there.

"George and I had been stumbling along, with things going from bad to worse," she would recall years later in her book. "He never talked about it but I believe that after that night he found Eric and I together, I think he felt he could be as blatant as he liked in his pursuit of other women."

Pattie was feeling vulnerable and alone about Harrison and the marriage. All of which lead to a literal merry-go-round of affairs on both sides of the relationship. Harrison had an extended relationship with Krissie, the wife of Small Faces' guitarist Ronnie Wood, who much like the Eric Clapton situation he had befriended and were working together, while Pattie ended up sleeping with Wood, all of which was chronicled in Wood's memoir *Ronnie: The Autobiography*.

"I had a heartfelt and fiery affair with George Harrison's wife, Pattie. One night at George's house I took George aside and told him quite seriously that when it was time for bed I would be going to Pattie's room. Seemingly unflustered, he pointed to the room Krissie and I were staying in, and said, 'I shall be sleeping there. When the time came, the two of us were left standing on the landing, hands on the doorknobs of our respective rooms and in we went. Pattie was surprised to see me. I told her that I thought she was seriously neglected, was going to waste and that I felt strongly about her. The next morning we were awakened by George. Pattie and I went off to The Bahamas and George and Krissie left for Portugal."

To this day, Pattie steadfastly denies the Wood affair ever happened, offering in *TheAge.com* that "Eric was my first and only infidelity."

The affair with Wood did not last long but it seemed to open Pattie up to the notion of having other relationships while still in what had become a loveless relationship with Harrison. Although it had been rumored for years, Pattie would vehemently deny that she had an affair with John Lennon. But there was evidence that given the opportunity, she would be agreeable to extramarital affairs if the opportunity presented itself.

In 1974, Pattie flew to Los Angeles to spend some time with her sister Jenny who, at the time, was married to Mick Fleetwood. While there, she reconnected with old friends Delaney and Bonnie Bramlett whose marriage, it turned out, was also in trouble at the time. She would spend a few days with Delaney and Bonnie. In the book *Behind Sad Eyes: The Life of George Harrison*, Delaney recalled that during those conversations, he sensed that Pattie and Harrison might be having difficulties but being a true gentleman it was not in his nature to pry.

One day, Pattie asked Delaney to drive her back to her hotel so she could get a change of clothes. It seemed like an innocent request. But as they drove to the hotel, the singer would get an unexpected surprise. "She said she was only going to change clothes," Delaney said in the book *Behind Sad Eyes*. "But all of a sudden she started coming onto me in an aggressive romantic way. She was just very friendly, let me put it to you that way."

Things were on the verge of getting out of control when Delaney stopped it cold. "If it hadn't been for my friendship with George, something would have happened," he said in *Behind Sad Eyes*. "But I wasn't about to do anything that would harm our friendship. I think Pattie gathered that when I would bring up George's name every two seconds and made some excuse about having to get back to the studio. I think she was a little upset that I was not responding to her. I think she thought I didn't think she was attractive or something."

The trip to Los Angeles had been a breakthrough for Pattie. In her quiet moments she was discovering that she was tired of the games, the dishonesty and, perhaps most important, how she had been neglecting her own best emotional interest and feelings. She had been scheduled to fly back to London but, at the last possible moment, she flew instead to Florida where Clapton was recording his latest album. They were happy to see each other. Then it was time to lay their cards on the table.

Pattie admitted that she had been manipulating Clapton in order to recapture Harrison's love but that was now finally over Harrison and wanted to be with him. Clapton, not widely known for expressing his innermost feelings, agreed with Pattie's notion that they had been drawn together because of their loneliness and neediness. And that they had now finally realized that the love they felt for each other was real.

Both knew that the next step was dealing with Harrison. Pattie returned to London where she told Harrison that she was again with Clapton and that she would not be coming back to him. Harrison's response was "It's no big deal."

For Clapton, the challenge would be different. He and Harrison had remained close friends throughout and, being quite principled, he felt he had to deal with the issue face to face. The opportunity presented itself during a party for the release of Clapton's new album. Harrison was there. At one point, Clapton went up to Harrison and said, 'I'm in love with your wife. What are you going to do about it?' Harrison's response was 'Whatever you like man. It doesn't worry me.'"

Pattie witnessed the whole thing and, according to a quote from Clapton from the book *Behind Sad Eyes: The Life of George Harrison*, she was stunned. "Pattie freaked out and ran away. Suddenly she was in limbo. George must have been very upset too. But that's crazy! If he didn't want her to leave him, he shouldn't have let me take her."

This confrontation would be the proverbial last nail in the coffin of the marriage of Pattie and Harrison. She was now free, in every possible way, to be with Clapton. Divorce proceedings took three years to wind their way through the court system until a final decree was signed in 1977. Pundits would point to the divorce as being one of the most amicable they had ever seen. So much so that Pattie, in conversation with *McCartneyTimes.com* would still wax nostalgic of her time with Harrison. "I think George was very loving. Even after we split, he was always my friend. We'd speak on the phone all the time."

From the time Pattie and Clapton officially became an item, she was experiencing a sense of déjà vu. There was a sense of excitement in Pattie, much like there had been in the early days of her relationship with Harrison. Both men were alike, introverted, by degrees sensitive. They were ego driven and highly creative and so totally unpredictable. But much like her relationship with Harrison, Pattie was taken with the fantasy of being with Clapton. "I had this wonderful, childlike belief that love would last forever," she offered *The Sydney Morning Herald*. Pattie would further acknowledge to *The Guardian* that "I fell into Eric's seductive trap and I believed it."

Indeed, it all seemed a bit of a fairy tale in the early days. With the love and support of Pattie, Clapton had gone into rehab and had emerged heroin free. In his newfound sobriety, Clapton offered Pattie an opportunity she had never had with Harrison, to accompany him on his 1974 US tour. Standing in the wings each night of the 26 city tour, Pattie would see her new love at his best, a master musician who could bring audiences to fits of ecstasy, especially when it came to the song that had touched Pattie so deeply, "Layla." But away from the concerts, Pattie saw Clapton at his worst.

"I found the tour exhausting," she recalled in her memoir *Wonderful Tonight*. "For Eric, after three years of heroin addiction, it was shattering. He coped by drinking. Eric had moved from heroin to alcohol without blinking. He began in the morning and drank all day until 4:00 when his minder forced him to stop drinking so he could have enough time to sober up before the show."

With the conclusion of the tour, Pattie and Clapton went on holiday to Jamaica. Pattie had hoped that time together away from the spotlight would get Clapton off the booze and back into her arms. Sadly she would be disappointed. In the romantic confines of Montego Bay, Pattie spent her days alone while Clapton smoked dope and drank nonstop into the evening, leaving Pattie alone in paradise eating dinner alone.

"In my naivety, I believed everything was alright," she said in *The Telegraph*. "He wasn't taking heroin, which I thought was the main addiction for him. But, as it turned out, the drug of choice turned out to be alcohol."

The couple would return to Clapton's home in Surrey where Pattie found her most peaceful moments roaming the massive gardens. But as she quickly discovered, life with Clapton was not much different than life with Harrison had been.

"Life was like one big party fueled by alcohol," she related in her book *Wonderful Tonight*. "We were like a couple of children playing at being grown-ups." Clapton could be generous financially and, most important, emotionally to Pattie. She has often looked back fondly at the night he wrote the song "Wonderful Tonight" while waiting for her to dress for an evening out. "That song was a poignant reminder of all that was good in our relationship," she said in her book. "And when things went wrong it was torture to hear it."

Almost immediately, things began to go wrong. Clapton had become a full-blown alcoholic, needing to consume massive amounts of alcohol every five hours. "I was madly in love with him but as I negotiated his moods and the destructiveness that went with his drinking, I began to wonder if I had made a mistake in leaving George," she admitted in her book *Wonderful Tonight*.

Pattie's fears would be confirmed at one point when Clapton began getting too friendly with a model friend of Pattie's named Jenny McClain. The two would often be found together by Pattie in their house in compromising situations that, at one point, upset Pattie to the point where she went to Los Angeles to stay with her sister and try to figure out what was going on with her relationship and her life.

"I felt a complete fool," Pattie chronicled in her book and in excerpts in *The Daily Mail*. "I had given up George for this. I spent several weeks with friends in Los Angeles. I had no plans to see Eric again."

Pattie would admit in an interview with *The Telegraph* that her personality seemed the perfect magnet for self-centered men who would use and abuse her. "I was a very shy person and, I suppose, easily manipulated. It's quite understandable to realize that you are the subject of desire and that's quite a passive thing to be."

By late March 1979, Pattie was ready to end her relationship with Clapton when she received an unexpected call from his manager/minder. He was relaying the message that Clapton wanted to get married on Tuesday, in Tucson, Arizona, just before the start of his latest American tour. There was a not too veiled threat in the message that, in essence, if Pattie didn't marry Clapton, the relationship was over.

Pattie hung up the phone and weighed her options. She kept returning to the comparisons between Clapton and Harrison. "The drink was a problem," she said in an excerpt from her book published in *The Daily Mail*. "But other than that he was wonderful. He was the most exciting, creative, talented, interesting person. And I was in love with him."

Pattie called up Clapton and, once he had assured her that Jenny was no longer in the picture, she agreed to marry him. Pattie and Clapton were married on March 27 at The Apostolic Assembly of Faith Church in Christ Jesus. Pattie looked back on the service as a happy moment. Within a week, her happy moment would come crashing down.

The memory of Clapton bringing Pattie on stage the opening night of the tour and singing the song "Wonderful Tonight" was quickly dashed days later when Clapton told Pattie he wanted her to go home because, as it turned out, Jenny was checking into a hotel during an upcoming tour stop for yet another rendezvous. "Eric and I hadn't even been married a week and Jenny was back," she said in a *Daily Mail* excerpt from her book. "And stupidly, perhaps, I chose to be forgiving."

But while forgiving, Pattie was also coming to grips with the realities of the man she had married. "Eric loves himself," she declared in *The McCartney Times.com.* "I don't think there was ever much room for me."

And knowing this may well have been an overriding factor in Pattie letting herself go. She would often appear tired, bedraggled and was putting on weight, her face noticeably puffy. "I was drinking far more than was good for me," she offered in *Wonderful Tonight.* "But I always felt I was in control of my drinking."

The downhill slide of the marriage reached critical mass in 1980 when Clapton began to suffer the ravages of years of alcohol addiction. In 1980, she stood by as Clapton was admitted to a hospital, suffering from a total of five ulcers. Doctors strongly suggested that he give up drinking to no avail. In 1982, Clapton finally admitted he had a drinking problem and checked himself into a rehab center. He would emerge six weeks later, allegedly cured of his desire to drink but that only lasted six months before the pressures of touring and life drove him back to drink. Pattie would witness what Clapton in the throes of alcoholism had become—somebody she now feared.

"There were times when he was more like an animal than the loving husband I had known," she said in *Wonderful Tonight.* "I was frightened. I thought he'd end up killing one of us."

But Pattie would continue to stand by her man, flaws and all as she offered in conversation with *ABC News.* "The relationship [with Clapton] was all about extremes. Loads of heartache and loads of fun."

Adding to the mounting wreckage of the marriage was the fact that, as with Harrison, Pattie and Clapton had been trying for years to have a child. And also like with Harrison, they were not successful. Through all the glitz and glamour Pattie, in her heart, always felt the pangs for motherhood and it was a feeling that became stronger as she got older. "I was in my 30's and ready to have babies," she admitted to *The Sydney Morning Herald*. "I used to wander around the house, thinking to myself 'this will be the baby's room and the nanny can sleep here'"

When she was younger and still with Harrison, Pattie had not been overly concerned with motherhood, always assuming that, as she offered in *StartsAt60.com*, "that it would happen one day." But as her relationship with Clapton progressed over a five-year period and they continued to not conceive, Pattie began to get concerned. "

It had not been for want of trying. Pattie and Clapton were both keen on having children. "It never occurred to me that it wouldn't be possible," Pattie lamented in *StartsAt60.com*. "I just thought that it would happen sometime. Then it just didn't."

Uncharacteristically, Clapton was wildly attentive and supportive when it came to the issue of the couple having children. Although he was dead set against the couple adopting (as had been Harrison), he was there for Pattie as she went to several doctors and endured two in vitro fertilization procedures that, sadly, resulted in two miscarriages. Pattie acknowledged her sense of frustration in *StartsAt60.com* when she said, "I really tried and still nothing happened. I thought 'I have to get my head around this.'"

Unbeknownst to Pattie, Clapton was psychologically devastated at the couple remaining childless and, in his constant alcoholic state, had set a drastic course to remedy the problem. Pattie began hearing reports of numerous Clapton infidelities during recent tours. That coupled with his incessant drinking that often found him passed out in front of her, Pattie had finally had enough. In September 1984 she walked out, staying with her mother for a while before getting her own flat in London. Clapton would show up at her house on a couple of occasions looking thin, shaking and obviously suffering from the DT's, begging her to come back to him. Finally, Pattie put her foot down.

"I told him 'No, you're still drinking. I can't do it.'"

Pattie was seemingly resolute in establishing a new life. She began looking up old friends she had not seen in years, began to indulge herself once again as a photographer and, perhaps as a way of getting back at Clapton, embarked on a short lived affair with photographer Will Christie. If Christie would be her rebound relationship, he would stand in stark deference to both Clapton and Harrison. She found him easy to be with, always upbeat and no pressure whatsoever. Pattie would often remember her time with Christie as being the first time in years that she felt cherished. It did not come as a surprise that Pattie fell quickly and deeply in love. For his part, Christie had little to say about his time with Pattie, other than to tell *The Times* that his time with Pattie was "magical."

However, the emotional tussle between Pattie and Clapton would continue. Clapton begged Pattie for forgiveness and another chance. Pattie went back to Clapton and all seemed bliss for a short period of time before Clapton departed on a European tour. In the spirit of transparency, Clapton returned from the tour and informed Pattie that he had met a girl named Lory Del Santo and that they had slept together a couple of times. Almost as an afterthought, Clapton proclaimed that he was still in love with Pattie but that he thought he was also in love with Del Santo. All of which put the ever-tolerant Pattie on the horns of yet another dilemma. "I could put up with infidelity," she related in *Wonderful Tonight*. "It was purely physical. Sex was no threat to our marriage. Emotion was a different matter."

Pattie was hurt and disappointed at Clapton's lack of morals and propriety but managed to put this latest affair out of her mind. There would remain an uneasy tension between the couple through the remainder of 1984. Pattie was not sure which way to turn but her love for Clapton, flaws and all, remained her go-to emotion. Until, during a private Christmas dinner, Clapton would drop yet another bombshell. Del Santo was pregnant.

For Pattie, this was the last straw. She acknowledged her anger in a passage from *Wonderful Tonight*. "I told Eric I didn't want to share a bed with him anymore and that I didn't want to sleep with him again."

The last tattered remains would drag on through 1987. Clapton and Del Santo's child, a boy named Connor, was born in August 1986 amid Clapton's fantasy scenario that he and Pattie would stay married and that she would be part of Connor's life. All of this was taking place while Pattie was attempting yet another in vitro fertilization procedure that she hoped would be successful and that Clapton and she could, somehow, make a go of it. Complications arose when Del Santo, angry at Clapton's attempt to insinuate Pattie into her child's life, left Clapton and returned to Italy where Clapton would make sporadic visits.

Pattie continued to suffer in silence the inevitable trips by Clapton to visit his son and his bubbly good news of the latest discovery of fatherhood. The pain cut deep into her heart, as did the fact that Clapton had continued to drink and his moods and temper would darken. It would be one of Clapton's drunken fits, coincidentally on the morning of Pattie's 43rd birthday, that she would recall in *Wonderful Tonight* that would end it all.

"He burst into my bedroom at six in the morning in a drunken rage and told me to get out. He was screaming obscenities at me and accused me of not being a proper wife because I wouldn't sleep with him. Then he threw my things out the window. I picked up my things from the drive, got into my car and drove to London. I knew I had to get out for his sake as well as mine. We had to divorce."

The divorce decree was granted in 1989. The press had a field day with the news, much to Pattie's embarrassment. Clapton's alcohol and past drug problems were on display, as was his countless affairs, his illegitimate son (a second out of wedlock child, with a woman named Ruth which would also surface in the court proceedings). Pattie was awarded the divorce and a modest amount of money in the settlement. But as she would recall in *Wonderful Tonight*, no amount of money was going to salve the damage done to her psychologically.

"I was so utterly distraught. I've never been so upset, confused and unhappy in all my life. I was totally confused as to who I was." She would also acknowledge years later in conversation with *The Telegraph* that the divorce had caused her severe psychological damage. "It probably took me six years to get over it and four of those years were spent in psychotherapy. My self-esteem was unbelievably low. I found it hard to build up relationships because I had been so used to being with difficult people. Anybody who was sweet and nice to me was no challenge."

Being on her own also brought about the challenges of a new lifestyle. No longer a member of the pop music elite, Pattie was, while comfortable, adjusting to such compromises as taking public transportation as opposed to private limos and airplanes. It was to Pattie's credit that she quickly adjusted to the fact that she was now on her own and had to do something to make a living. She had long had a reputation as being a first rate amateur photographer after years of shooting up close and personal candid's of rock stars and celebrities in the 60's and now, with much support from a tightknit group of old friends, decided to turn professional.

Which as she recalled in *TheMortonReport.com* would require a bit of on the job training. "I've always been basically self-taught and then I realized that I didn't really understand the mechanics of the camera. So I had three months of lessons with a very sweet elderly couple. I'd go twice a week to them and I learned darkroom techniques and more intricate ways of taking photographs."

Pattie learned her lessons well and soon embarked on a late in life career as a commercial photographer for magazines as well as more informal but no less intimate photos of children. Her work would also go on to head several photo exhibits in international galleries and brought no small amount of critical praise for an aesthetic that is equal parts professional and feminist.

"I will not take a photograph of somebody in a bad pose or not looking good," she explained in *TheMortonReport.com*. "The reason being is that I always hated seeing horrible pictures of myself and was always confused. How come the photographer didn't notice that I was looking kind of odd or not sitting properly? I can tell by looking at a photograph if it's taken by a woman. I think there's a sensitivity and also a kind of attention to detail or the color or the human qualities that a woman can see more clearly than a man."

With the exception of an alleged 'very short relationship' (whose identity remains a mystery to this day) on the heels of her divorce from Clapton, Pattie spent the ensuing years finding herself personally and professionally and reflecting on the fact that she had become not only a survivor but somebody very much in touch with her inner self. "I feel that I've finally shrugged off my insecurities and the idea that it's okay that I was Mrs. George and Mrs. Eric and that I can actually now feel proud that I'm now doing something that I'm feeling quite proud of and that I really enjoy doing," she said in *TheMortonReport.com*."

During this period of life as a now twice-divorced semi-celebrity of sorts, Pattie would still be approached by the media about when she would again consider becoming romantically involved. Initially her response would be curt and evasive but, as she moved on in her life, she would become more forthcoming on the subject, as witnessed in an interview with *The Guardian*. "I don't know if one has choices about men or whether life is mapped out for us and you meet somebody and there's chemistry and that's it. You think you've chosen them, but maybe you were meant to be with them anyway. But I do know that I wouldn't go for somebody now who drinks too much. I'd like to go for a man who is a grown up. But there are not many of them. That's why I'm on my own."

Pattie would be on holiday with friends in Sri Lanka in the late 80's when she met Rod Weston, a successful property developer who was nine years younger than she was. The two got along quite well and stayed in touch over the years before actually starting to date in 1994. Sparks flew once again for Pattie and Weston and she they live together in bliss until they decided to make it all legal by getting married in 2015. With Weston, Pattie had seemingly found the ideal mate for this point in her life.

"He is very supportive, comfortable to be with and, yes, very good-looking," she told *Hello Magazine.* "I realized that I could actually stand up to a man and he wasn't going to desert me." She would also acknowledge the third time being the charm in conversation with *The Sydney Morning Herald.* "We have a nice relationship that's warm and friendly with no pressure. That is a relief."

Now well into her 70's and the lone surviving first generation Beatle wife, Pattie is living the calm, serene and very un-rock n' roll life. But that does not mean she has left her life as a muse to great musicians behind. She heard from Harrison on occasion and spoke to him shortly before his death. The consensus of those conversations was they had made peace and that Harrison in his final years acknowledged that he had not treated her well. Less amicable has been the communication between Pattie and Clapton. She had moments with him at parties that were, at best, cursory and fleeting and did not involve their turbulent past.

She has also chosen to meet the reality of her life with those two creative giants with two books that lay bare her life with Harrison and Clapton, *Wonderful Today* (2007) and *Wonderful Tonight: George Harrison, Eric Clapton and Me* (2008). Sporadically she has spoken to the media about those times but, in recent years, has grown tired of rehashing the same stories over and over again and has retreated into a life of contentment and peace.

But occasionally, given the right moment or mood, she will venture back into those times and what made her the legendary muse that inspired great songs, as was the case when she consented yet again to diagnose the reality of it all during an interview with *The Telegraph.*

"Maybe it had more to do with them than it did me," she speculated. "Perhaps Eric just wanted what George had. I don't really know for sure at this point. But what I do know is that it's amazing that we've all come through this and we're all still alive."

Chapter Four
Linda Eastman/McCartney

In the pantheon of Beatle wives, Linda McCartney may well be the most difficult to put a finger on. Not so much because she's elusive, ego-driven, or because, quite simply, she does not have a whole lot to say. To the contrary, she is quite the opposite. And because she happened to marry a Beatle, the process of pinning down just who Linda was has been, to many, a difficult proposition to say the least.

There is a lot that sets Linda apart from the first generation of Beatle wives. She was the first American-born wife. Her upbringing was more middle to upper class than working class. She had a significant career on a fairly large stage before meeting Paul. Oh, and lest we forget, she was Jewish. Throw in her seemingly lack of pretense and a bullshit factor that is quite low to nonexistent and a wide array of interests other than being Mrs. McCartney. But even she would concede, in that rare interview moment in 1989 with the *San Diego Union Tribune*, that there are advantages to being a Beatle wife most people tend to forget is there.

"I'm one of those people who will say what I want to say and do what I want to do. For me, it's easy because I am ordinary. I really am down to earth. I love nature. I love animals and I love my freedom. In fact, that's the exciting part... being free."

That Linda was born into the upper class of American society immediately set her apart from the first incarnation of Beatle wives who sprang from lower class, blue collar roots. But she has often acknowledged that she was out of sync with the notion of being upper class and financially secure. She would make that very plain in conversation with *Playgirl*. "There's nothing wrong with living in the grand manner. But I was never comfortable with it. I found it pretentious and shallow. I never liked having servants around. It's not just an invasion of your privacy, after a while you begin to feel like they own you."

And she further acknowledged in the *San Diego Union Tribune* interview that part of being contrary to the clichés of society and class in her world is the ability to say no to the almost prerequisite requirement of a Beatle wife to do boatloads of press. "I rarely do interviews and I request not to do too many. I felt for a long time that I had nothing to really sell or say. But now I have things to say so I'm doing them. I'm not a show biz person. But I married somebody in showbiz. Why mention me other than that I am the wife?"

Linda was Jewish when being Jewish as the war with Germany was raging was not always looked upon in a positive manner. And that was very much on the mind of Lee Eastman—her parents were Leopold Vail Epstein and Louise Sarah Linder according to the book *Fab: An Intimate Life of Paul McCartney* by Howard Sounes. Louise had come from prominence and money as the daughter of Max J. Linder, a noted German-Jew who had made his fortune and prestige as a clothing manufacturer in Cleveland. Consequently, when she fell in love with a New York entertainment lawyer named Lee Eastman who had changed his name from Leopold Vail Epstein, convinced that life would be easier if he presented as being less Jewish, Louise's family was convinced that she was making a mistake and marrying beneath her.

But marry they did and by the time Linda Louise Eastman was born on September 24, 1941, the die had been cast around the notion that if people asked there was no problem admitting they were Jewish but, otherwise, it was best not to advertise the fact. However, Lee and Louise did not renounce their religion and, in the privacy of their own home, did their best to keep their faith. "I think my parents tried to have something for Passover once," she said in the book *Linda McCartney: A Portrait*, "and we all made fun of it."

And it would often be through her parent's attempts at being Jewish and yet not Jewish that informed Linda's early anti-religious sentiments. She was far from being an atheist and would readily admit to "being all Jewish" in the book *Linda McCartney: The Biography* in which she projected a view of organized religion that was suspect at best. "I've always hated religion. It's the most guilt ridden, horrible thing. 'My God is better than yours and I'm going to fight you and kill you because of your religion.' I think it's just a sick idea."

Linda would grow into a child of privilege at a very early age, living in a house in the posh East Hamptons and a Park Avenue apartment. Her father's clients, a who's who of artists like Willem De Kooning, Franz Kline and songwriter Jack Lawrence were always in and out of her home and, in one story that have lived on forever, Linda's father persuaded Lawrence to write a song for his then four year-old daughter called *"Linda"* which would go on to be a commercial hit in the 1940's. Many historians have speculated that "Linda" was the first step toward Linda feeling her first real sense of importance and, perhaps, superiority.

As she grew older, the at large impression was that Linda would become part of the latest generation of high society girls. Years later Paul McCartney, in an excerpt of an interview that appeared in *Lilith Magazine.org*, would say there was nothing further from the truth. "She came from a strata of society which was really, probably, American aristocracy and she never really valued it. She thought it had a lot of false values, that there was a lot of social climbing and she never wanted that."

But she would concede that through all the high society pretentions she experienced from an early age, her parents were just the right fit for her and for the times. "My father was a very bright man, He was from a peasant background and yet so astute, so smart," she reflected in *Linda McCartney: The Biography*. "My mother was attentive and charming… everybody loved her."

It would become evident in Linda's formative years that formal education was not of much interest. She had a hard time paying attention in class and would often be reprimanded by teachers for staring dreamily out of a classroom window. "I didn't read books because I was always more interested in what was going on around me than words in a book," she said in an interview with the radio station Oobu Joobu.com. "So teachers thought I was a bit of a wise apple."

Her disinterest in school would also regularly have the young girl on the receiving end of a scolding by her father. Like many upscale families of the time, Lee had visions of his daughter following in his footsteps, going on to university and following him in a career in law. But by the time Linda matriculated to *Scarsdale High School*, Lee had all but given up the notion that his daughter would go into the legal profession.

Linda was candid in conversation with *Playgirl* in assessing her lack of ambition as it related to the Eastman lineage. "I come from a very academic family. My father was brilliant. My brother was brilliant. They both went to *Harvard Law School* and did very well. All I ever cared about was animals, rock music and photography."

By the time she had reached her teens, Linda had become a very outdoors person, exploring the city's woods and streams and marveling at the wonders of nature. "Scarsdale was country when I was a kid," she explained to *Fame* magazine. "It was farm country. Everyone thinks I'm this spoiled Westchester girl but I'm not. I'm a country lover and a nature lover."

The yin and yang of Linda's high school years were evident by the fact that, while her attitude toward not reading and studying was legendary, she had evolved into an award-winning horsewoman. Those accomplishments aside, Linda spent those years largely invisible. It was known that she loved to sing and that not being very good at it never stopped her from trying again. And it went without saying that many was the night when she was supposed to be at the library studying, she was in fact hanging out with her friends, listening to the latest songs by The Kingston Trio and The Everly Brothers.

"All my teen years were spent with my ear to the radio," she said in an excerpt from a feature in *The Hitchhiker's' Guide to the Galaxy: Earth Edition.com*.

By 1959, the then 17-year-old Linda was being pressured. It was time for all proper upper class girls to pick a prestigious university. Linda would always make the point that colleges of that caliber did not offer degrees in nature, horses, art and rock n'roll, the only things she was truly interested in. But Linda's parents continued to pressure her. And so largely to appease them, Linda chose the path of least effort, by enrolling in the University of Arizona in Tucson. It may have seemed like compromise but, as she offered in *Playgirl*, "I guess I rebelled against the privilege I was born into. I felt I had been pressured by men all my life. I rather liked the idea of being on my own, making my own decisions."

Her tenure at the *University of Arizona* was half hearted at best. She sleepwalked through her classes, exhibiting the same sense of aimlessness and lack of goal that had become a constant in her life. She would spend more time riding horses in the Arizona desert than studying and becoming romantically involved with a geology student named Joseph Melvin See. Her short-term plan had been to major in art history but she essentially dropped out of school before choosing a major. Linda's father was livid, threatening to pull all financial support if she was not in school. Pushed into a corner, a desperate Linda thrashed about for a way to make a living on her own for the first time.

"Alright, I'll be a dental assistant, I said to myself" she recalled in *Linda McCartney: The Biography*. "But I went for one interview and I thought 'Oh my God! No way!'"

It would be at Linda's lowest emotional point that fate stepped in. On a whim, she decided to attend an evening photography class at the Tucson Arts Center. "The instructor was an older woman in a wheelchair," she recalled in an interview with *The Morning Call*. "And there were the most fantastic photographs by the photographers Walker Evans, Dorothea Lange, Ansel Adams and Henri Cartier Bresson. They totally captivated me. At the end of the night the instructor said 'take your roll of film and I'll see you next week.' I went up to her and said 'I don't have a camera.' And she said 'Well borrow one.' So I did. I took photos of the mountains, a horse, a kid and all that kind of stuff. Next week, I brought a contact sheet to class. She looked at it and was really impressed. I said 'I don't know anything about photography,' and she said, 'It doesn't matter, you've got a good eye.' I never went back to class. I just started taking pictures and it all fell into place."

Linda jumped into photography with a passion and soon found a side of herself she had never known as she offered in a look back in *The Hitchhiker's Guide to the Galaxy: Earth Edition*. "Photography made me a different person because it was something I loved doing and just nothing else mattered."

Linda was in the process of finally finding herself on a number of emotional and life levels when tragedy struck. On March 1, 1962 American Airlines Flight 1, carrying 95 passengers on a routine flight from New York to Los Angeles, crashed shortly after takeoff. There were no survivors. Linda's mother was one of those passengers. Linda immediately flew back to New York to be with her family.

"I had never really connected with my mother," Linda, still devastated and guilty years later, reflected in a *Vanity Fair* interview. "But for my father, it had been a disaster. My parents had been so very much in love."

After 'being there' for her family at this tragic moment, Linda's thoughts were at loose ends which resulted in a fateful decision. She returned to Arizona. She would be candid with *Vanity Fair* in stating that the decision was not very well thought out. "It was a mistake. It was kind of escapism. I was very immature. I just escaped."

Back to Arizona where she immediately turned to her boyfriend See for comfort. Within a matter of weeks, Linda discovered she was pregnant. The couple did the right thing and was married on June 18, 1962. A daughter, Heather, was born December 31, 1962. It was almost an understatement to say that from the moment the couple said their 'I do's, Linda knew she had made a mistake. They were young and as they quickly discovered, they had totally dissimilar lifestyles. See, who would soon graduate with a degree in Geo Physics, was a hardcore academic who spent most of his time studying and researching. Linda found herself preferring a less intellectual/naturalistic lifestyle, no doubt fueled by her growing passion for photography. The marriage simply was not working and, less than a year in, she found herself hopelessly unhappy.

The last straw for Linda came shortly after See graduated when he announced he was going to Africa to do further study and research. As she recalled in *Linda McCartney: A Biography* she sat her husband down and laid her cards on the table. "I said, 'look, if I don't get on with you here, I'm not going to Africa with you. I won't get with you there.'"

See went to Africa alone and Linda suddenly found herself a single mother with no prospect for a job, but suddenly feeling as free as a bird. "While he was in Africa, I met somebody that I liked a whole lot better," she said in her biography. "So I wrote him and said I was getting a divorce. I got a letter back from him saying 'Let's not.' I said 'Yeh, come on, let's get a divorce.' Luckily he agreed."

The divorce was finalized in June 1965. By that time, Linda had moved to Tucson, fallen in with a bunch of like-minded bohemians and artists and juggling being a single mother with a photographer on a creative mission. "When my marriage broke up, I just decided to get away from everything I had ever known," she related in *Hitchhiker's Guide to the Galaxy: Earth Edition*. "I was staying with friends and spending a lot of time riding around on the edge of the desert."

Encouraged by her growing proficiency with a camera, her very first sale of a British actor who had passed through Tucson to *Spotlight Magazine* and the fantasy of using photography as a way to make a living, she packed up Heather and returned to New York.

Linda stayed with her father (who had since remarried) for a time before deciding, with a gentle push from her father, to own all the decisions she had made and move, and moved out on her own. Her mother had left her a bit of money but New York, at that point, was already expensive and so she settled for a $180 a month rental on the

Upper East Side which was not far removed from a lifestyle she had been running from. "Maybe if I had known the city better I would have gone downtown," she chuckled in the book *Linda McCartney: A Biography*. Now there was just the little matter of finding a job.

Linda had once taken a typing class and used that element of a truly skimpy resume to land a job as a receptionist at *Town & Country* magazine at the princely sum of $65 a week. Linda was now officially a part of the workaday grind. She would get up early each morning, take Heather to a nursery on the West Side, catch a bus to her job on the East Side by 9:00 and, at the stroke of 5:00, rush back across town to pick up Heather. She had no social life during those early days but, on the rare occasion she was out, Heather was never far from her mind. "Mainly I had a daughter," she said in an excerpt from a 1992 interview that appeared in *Linda McCartney: A Biography*. "I had to be home at night. I was a straight girl but a little bit funky."

Those early days of struggling had put Linda in a strange psychological state, truly on her own and facing the challenges of a working woman and single mother, coupled with odd eating habits, lots of crackers and snacks, Linda would comes across to outsiders like photographer David Dalton, as energetic but depressed. Dalton formed that impression one night in 1965 when he was on an assignment at a club called *The Scene*. "I had just finished taking my photos when a tall girl with long blonde hair came up to me and began asking a lot of questions," he recalled in a *Gadfly Online* story. "Did I do this for a living? How does one get into this? Is it hard to learn? You could tell she was educated, smart and hungry. She had this wonderful name, Linda See."

Dalton agreed to mentor Linda's budding photo career, which in turn, would lead to a somewhat short-lived romantic relationship. He would take her along on jobs shooting rock musicians and she met her first real rock stars, The Animals and The Dave Clark Five (the latter group which is credited on Linda's official website as being her first rock star photos.)

Linda's mind was always seemingly on the move, thinking about what could be next. Part of her job at *Town & Country* was to route incoming mail to the appropriate staffers. There were always invitations to press junkets and parties coming across her desk. In June 1966, a particular invite caught her attention. The Rolling Stones were in America to hype their upcoming album *Aftermath* and were holding a meet and greet aboard the yacht *SS Sea Panther*. As she would recall in a *BBC* interview, "I opened the invitation and thought 'Well I'll do that one.'"

Linda arrived at the appointed time, camera and lots of film at hand, and was mingling with the assembled journalists and photographers when the event publicist approached her. "She came up to me and said 'Well we don't have room for all the photographers and journalists so you will be the only photographer on the boat," she continued her *BBC* telling. "I thought 'Oh my God! I'm not really a photographer! Does she know?' But I bluffed my way on. I mean I really didn't bluff it. I figured it was her (the publicists) choice. So I got on the boat, had a lot of film with me, and started shooting. I think my only worry was that the pictures wouldn't turn out. I was a bit shy and introverted through it all but, looking out through the lens, I saw and forgot myself and could actually see life. The enthusiasm was suddenly coming out of me and photography suddenly changed my life in that way. It wasn't just The Rolling Stones. It was the whole thing."

By the end of the day, Linda had connected with many journalists on the junket and her photos would end up being used to illustrate a number of features. Even *Town & Country*, whose editorial tastes tended to run more to upper crust than rock n'roll, would devoted several pages in the coming issue to a pictorial of Linda's photos of The Rolling Stones. Linda's newfound talent immediately translated into rock n'roll royalty.

Her ability to interact and relate with often temperamental rock stars in a way that put them at ease made her the ideal choice to shoot musicians for magazines and newspapers all over the world. The likes of Neil Young, Jimi Hendrix, Bob Dylan and countless others welcomed Linda into their world over the next couple of years. *Life Magazine* commissioned her to shoot a cover photo of Jim Morrison. Linda would travel on assignment to San Francisco to shoot the band Big Brother And The Holding Company and would take a series of riveting photos of Janis Joplin. In 1967, her efforts were rewarded with honors as *Top Female Photographer of the Year*. The following year a photo of Eric Clapton would result in her being the first female photographer to have a cover photo in *Rolling Stone*.

Linda's photographic style had become much talked about in terms of her technique. But Linda, in a *BBC* interview, acknowledged that what she did behind the lens was more a feel than anything else. "I think you feel it instinctively. You've got to just click on the moment, not before it and not after it. It just comes from my inners."

Along with her rapid rise to rock photographer to the stars would come an inevitable backlash, much of which could be justified. Linda's approach to photography was a level of familiarity and intimacy with her subjects that, between 1966-68, often resulted in Linda having sexual trysts with her subjects and gave rise to such derogatory nicknames as "The Groping Groupie" and "Linda Starfucker." Among those names that regularly appear on a list of famous musicians whom she slept with were Mick Jagger, Jimi Hendrix, Graham Nash, Roger Daltrey and Tim Buckley, as well as the oft reported but never completely substantiated night she spent with John Lennon.

But in all fairness to Linda, the 20 or so musicians she had sex with over a period of two years went a lot deeper than promiscuity. Linda, like all young women coming of age in the swinging 60's, especially in London, sexual freedom was part of the scenery. Men and women would hook up spontaneously and then move on to the proverbial next. Bottom line, Linda fresh off a failed marriage and suddenly thrust into the rock n'roll lifestyle, was a willing participant and one with progressive views on the idea of marriage and divorce.

"I really think it comes down to whether you're happy or you're not," she offered in *Linda McCartney: The Biography*. "If you're not happy, you should split and get happy as individuals."

A little less liberal and, perhaps, a bit more calculating was Linda's seemingly endless search, to many observers of the scene, that she was looking for a rich, successful and creatively accomplished man to give her and her child security.

But in the meantime, Linda was living the dream as she chronicled in one of a series of recently discovered letters to friend Miki Antony, excerpts of which would be published in a number of outlets including *Happy Magazine.com*. "I quit my job at *Town & Country* magazine to become a freelance photographer. I sell mainly to teen magazines because most of my subjects are rock n' roll groups. It's so groovy. I have photographed many English groups. The Stones were my favorite. I went out with Mick Jagger. He's really a terrific person, much to my surprise."

In May 1967, Linda took on a more expansive assignment, to travel to England to shoot photos for an upcoming book entitled *Rock and Other Four Letter Words*. Still naïve about the way the fledgling industry worked, she had been elated when she was offered $10,000 to shoot the photos for the book but that the publisher ultimately only came up with $1,000. Linda was not happy, especially with author J. Marks, but would soldier on which, as she related in the book *Linda McCartney: A Biography,* would yet again put her in conflict with the wishes of her father.

"I spent the $1,000 on travelling and going to London," she recalled. "My father advised me not to do it. I said, 'Dad, I've got to do it. Don't tell me not to.' My father kept saying 'don't go to England' and I said 'I've absolutely got to go.' He was very unhappy about it."

She was being shown around the city by old friends, members of the group The Animals. For Linda, it was the ideal gig, being paid to hang out and shoot photos of rock stars. Nothing could beat that. As it would turn out something could. After watching a set by Georgie Fame and The Blue Flames. According to McCartney's account in the book *Many Years From Now, McCartney and Linda McCartney: A Biography*, McCartney spotted Linda from across the club. Linda remembered that, "We flirted a bit and then I had to go to the loo which meant I had to walk past Paul's table. He introduced himself and then said, 'We're going off to another club. Would you like to go?'" Linda said yes and they were soon off to *The Speakeasy* where during brief interludes McCartney discovered she was not the typical girl he was used to meeting. She was smart, obviously attractive in an unfashionable sort of way and, like McCartney, she had a passion for art and, in particular, the works of Rene Magritte.

On the pretense of showing Linda his own collection of Magritte paintings, the proposed after hours art viewing, which by this time included pop singer Lulu, ended up at McCartney's home for a late night get together. What happened between Linda and McCartney that night is open to conjecture. Some historians swear by the fact that Linda and McCartney made love that night. Lulu set the record straight in *Linda McCartney: A Biography* when she said, "They were very interested in each other. But Linda left Paul's home while the little gathering was still in progress."

Linda and Paul would meet up again four days later when she wrangled an invitation to a very tough ticket, a press conference for the release of The Beatles' *Sergeant Pepper's Lonely Hearts Club Band.* Linda, the professional, was all over the get together, snapping photos of The Beatles that would most certainly be in demand. But most importantly, Linda and McCartney managed some alone time away from the madness. Following the press conference, Linda was on a flight back to the states and a photo session with Steve Winwood's new group *Traffic*. But in her mind, she was a million miles away and, after spending little more than an hour with him amid the latest round of Beatlemania, she absolutely knew she was in love with McCartney.

Linda's fantasy was fueled over the next year by the occasional call from McCartney. It was evident that he was interested. But there was one fly in the ointment. McCartney was officially engaged to his long time girlfriend Jane Asher and the press was alive with the notion that the couple would soon be wed. Linda took the news and speculation in stride. For the moment she had more important things on her plate, motherhood and her work.

By the late 60's, Linda had established her already immense talent with a maximum amount of integrity and character. In the book *Linda McCartney: A Biography* Linda, in a 1992 interview, reflected back on her principles and do-it-yourself attitude. "I didn't have an agent. I didn't have an assistant. I didn't have anything. I did it all by myself on public transport. I guess that's what I would still be doing, taking pictures on an art level, on a satisfying level. I'd always have my own integrity. I'd always take pictures I believe in."

Lennon and McCartney flew to New York in May 1968 to promote the formation of the *Apple Corporation*. Linda and McCartney would use those days together at every opportunity and slowly but surely became a couple. Delving deep into the early days of their relationship, it was easy to see that there was much that brought them together. McCartney would often be effusive in the fact that he appreciated that Linda was beautiful in a naturalistic sort of way. She was creative, talented and worldly in her choices of art and music. She was a deep person who had come through life on her own terms and merits and so was not spoiled and materialistic.

In a personal sense, which was important to McCartney, who, like Linda, had been without a mother figure for much of his life, she was loving and supportive and all the things a man looks for in a potential mate. After their time in New York, they were apart for another three months, during which time Linda balanced out her emotional involvement with McCartney with a work a day life that included top of the mark photo sessions with the likes of Aretha Franklin and Judy Collins.

It was during the Aretha sessions that she received a phone call from McCartney, asking if she would fly to London to be with him. Emotionally Linda was all over the place as she confided to a close friend in a conversation that would appear in *Linda McCartney: A Biography*. "Do you think he says that to a lot of girls so that he is never without one?" she asked her friend. "He didn't say anything specific, just come over and call him when I get there. What if he wasn't serious?" And after a moment's hesitation, "Maybe I should go."

But not before she returned to New York and spent the next few weeks getting Heather in trusted hands and settling into her first year of school. It was a big moment for both of them and Linda, ever the dutiful mother, had to make sure her daughter would be safe before she set out on what she felt would be a turning point in her life.

By early September 1968, Linda was winging her way to London and whatever would lie ahead. At this point, McCartney and Jane Asher were no longer together. Linda's impact on being in McCartney's life was immediate. The physical and sexual compatibility was evident from the first days. But perhaps ultimately more important to the relationship was her ability to smooth out the rougher edges of his years as a bachelor. Not too subtle suggestions that he tidy up the house worked wonders on McCartney's sense of well-being.

Those in the know suggested that, given the ongoing tensions within The Beatles, McCartney was seen largely at peace when he was around her. They were like-minded when it came to music, art and nature. After years of countless relationships and affairs they had both suddenly found themselves in the ideal situation, the roles of boyfriend and girlfriend who were in love.

There would be some adjustments. The fact that Linda and McCartney were fairly open about the status of their live-in relationship was, in short order, making Linda the target of both the media and fans. The media avoided her in those early days. Fans were a different story.

Because she was American, many McCartney fanatics considered her an outsider who had swooped in and taken their fantasy away. Linda was immediately the target of verbal abuse, boo's and hisses, and not too veiled threats, often when she was in the company of McCartney. Initially, Linda ventured out of the home on her own but would immediately come under attack verbally and, in some cases, physically. Anti-Linda graffiti was also appearing in front of the McCartney home and there were several instances where rabid fans would break into the home and steal her photographs and negatives. It was not long before Linda had become a literal prisoner in the McCartney home, only venturing out in a car.

In an interview with author Danny Fields, elements of which would appear years later in Linda *McCartney A Biography*, would acknowledged those rough moments. "Those first few days in Paul's house I lived in fear of going outside. I was aware that I wasn't liked outside the home. I was scared of them. They really wished me harm. There was nothing I could do about the way they felt but they made me feel awful."

But amid the emotional turmoil, through it all, Linda and McCartney had fallen even deeper in love. He had been the ideal lover, kind, considerate and ever present in guiding Linda into the midst of this insane new world. Linda would be wistful as she offered author Fields the immediate loving nature of their relationship in those early days and months. "Paul and I loved each other. He told me he fell in love with me the first time we met. That was sweet of him to say whether it was true or not. What mattered to me was that he would always tell me that he was falling more and more in love with me as time went on."

The ease in which Linda ingratiated herself with the other Beatle wives was notable. The other women were at first bemused and tolerant but ultimately drawn to Linda. To their way of thinking she was not putting on airs. That she had become a recognized member of McCartney's life was much in evidence on the night The Beatles recorded the song "Birthday" and Linda was allowed to sing background vocals on the chorus, along with other Beatle wives.

Through those early weeks, Heather was never far from her mother's thoughts. They would speak by phone nightly. Linda's joy over her relationship with McCartney was tempered by the fact that Heather was not with them. Her daughter came up often in conversation and Linda's feeling was that McCartney was enthusiastic in including Heather in their lives. And so a decision was made.

Linda and McCartney hopped a plane for New York. The trip was clandestine and, to the couple's way of thinking to the point. They would do a bit of sightseeing. There was a large degree of anonymity by virtue of the fact that, with not too subtle prodding from Linda, McCartney was now sporting a beard and dressing down which was what the couple wanted. The important moments would be twofold. McCartney would meet Linda's parents and, most importantly, McCartney would meet Heather, which would be a smashing success. While in New York, McCartney, wearing his love for Linda in his heart and on his sleeve, broached the subject of marriage. Linda would recall the moment in a story in *Hitchhiker's Guide to the Galaxy: Earth Edition*.

"I really didn't want to get married again. I was so newly not married again. So I went 'no, no, no.' We kept walking and it was like it was never said."

But an important decision would be made during that visit. On October 31, 1968, Linda, McCartney and Heather winged their way back to London where they would live as a family. They would arrive back in London amidst chaos on a number of fronts. The anger by fans directed at Linda had reached a fever pitch and she was quite concerned about how Heather would handle the hostility. McCartney was facing stresses of his own, the disintegration of The Beatles on both a personal and professional level had turned into a constant battle of legal representatives and friendships fractured. By early November, the stresses had become too much and the family went to McCartney's second home, a farm in Scotland.

A place Linda had immediately fallen in love with as she offered in the book *Paul McCartney: Many Years From Now*. "Scotland was like nothing I had ever lived in. It was the most beautiful land you have ever seen, way at the end of nowhere. To me, it was the first feeling I had ever had of civilization dropping away."

The next few weeks would be idyllic. Linda found the country lifestyle and the relative seclusion to her liking and McCartney and Heather were continuing to bond, as he was continuing to show decidedly fatherly instincts. Linda would recall as much in conversation with author Fields. "Everything was going well for us, for the three of us."

Which was why in late November, while on holiday in Portugal, McCartney proposed marriage to Linda. She was still reluctant, the memories of her first marriage still lingered and she had already had a taste of what being a Beatle wife would entail. But McCartney reassured her that this time it would be all right. That's all it took to seal the deal. She said yes.

Linda and McCartney agreed that they just wanted a quiet wedding. But this being the height of Beatlemania, both knew that would not happen. The longstanding rumors of their impending marriage were laid to rest with a press release on March 11, 1969 that announced that Linda Eastman and Paul McCartney would be married on March 12 in a simple ceremony at Marylebone Registry Office in London. It would turn out to be anything but. In the hours leading up to the ceremony, police had to be called to quell a riot of upset fans that included an attempt to burn down McCartney's house. Linda and McCartney arrived through a back door of the registry office, a short ceremony ensued and the newly christened Mr. and Mrs. Paul McCartney emerged to the screaming of thousands of disappointed girls and a gaggle of press shouting questions and shooting pictures. Linda would take it well, acknowledging to a reporter for *The Daily Mail,* "Just write that the bride wore a big smile." And a big reason for the big smile may well have been that, unbeknownst to most, Linda was four months pregnant

After a whirlwind honeymoon and private time with both families, Linda and McCartney returned to married life made no less romantic but certainly at odds with the fact that The Beatles, legally and personally, were literally weeks away from calling it a day. The end of The Beatles would prove to be a truly messy affair. Lawsuits were flying between life-long friends, who had been choosing sides with McCartney being the odd man out. The birth of Mary McCartney on August 28, 1969 would be a momentary bright spot in the lives of the newlyweds.

McCartney was suffering deep depression and emotional torture as he watched his entire life unravel. Time away at their farm did little to ease his pain as Linda could do nothing but bear witness to the destruction of the man she loved. "I was very scared," Linda said of those dark days in an excerpt from the book *Linda McCartney: A Biography.* "I didn't want to give up. It was unreal and I had to handle all this by myself. We had two children and we'd just been married a year and my husband didn't want to get out of bed. He was drinking too much and he would tell me he was useless."

But through it all, Linda continued to tough it out and stand by her man. "If I knew what was coming would I have gone to London?" she offered in *Linda McCartney: A Biography.* "Would I have married him? Yes, of course I would have married Paul."

Linda knew McCartney well enough to know that his entire sense of self worth had been wrapped up in all things Beatles. Consequently she knew the only way to get him out of his funk was for him to go back to work. Her way of doing it was prototypical Linda, subtle as a train wreck and soft as butter. "I'm not a person who just gives up," she offered in *Playboy.* "I wouldn't think of [our situation] as 'Oh well, this is it.'" In an excerpt from the book *Man on the Run,* it was acknowledged by McCartney that Linda told him "Hey, you don't want to get too crazy." And when it came right down to it, Linda got in her husband's face and screamed, "Look! You're a grown man! You don't have to take this crap!"

McCartney finally got the message and, after an impromptu recording session during a visit to New York resulted in 21 songs, the couple returned to their farm in Scotland where, in a crude four track studio, McCartney recorded his first solo album entitled *McCartney*. The album would be a tentative DIY effort in which McCartney played all the instruments and a good number of the songs, specifically *"Maybe I'm Amazed"* were paeans to Linda and, what many deep thinkers speculated were veiled shots at his former friends in The Beatles.

When not looking after the children and taking care of running a household, Linda was very much a presence during the sessions, often contributing background vocals on many of the cuts. In a promotional interview inserted into the album, McCartney acknowledged Linda's contributions. "Strictly speaking she was a harmonizer but her contributions were much more than that. She was a shoulder to lean on, a second opinion. More than that, she believes in me."

McCartney would be largely dismissed by critics but would be somewhat successful internationally. Most importantly, the album had served to bring McCartney out of the dumps and he had emerged a much more peaceful person, dedicated to his family and the idea of keeping every aspect of his life simple after the chaos of The Beatles. When not riding around his property on horseback with his family, McCartney, by 1970, would regularly be found plucking out simple patterns on guitar. McCartney was suddenly finding a sense of religion in keeping things simple and it was with that in mind that he approached Linda with the idea of starting a band. In the same breath, he asked Linda if she would like to be in the band.

Linda was a bit gobsmacked at the suggestion that, with lots of desire but seemingly little or no musical talent, she could be in a band. With more than a little trepidation, and as reported years later in a documentary on the making of the album *Ram*, said "Uh, yeah."

Linda would eventually discover what her two-word agreement would entail. McCartney wanted his wife to be a functioning member of the band and not just eye candy. Under his guidance, Linda would learn the basics of playing keyboards. She would also take a larger role in the area of backing vocals and harmonies. But Linda could not have imagined that McCartney had envisioned his second solo album, *Ram*, as a vinyl monument to their love and relationship as an album by Paul and Linda McCartney in which Linda would receive co-songwriting credit on six songs.

"I didn't really think too much about it," she told *Playboy*. "I always thought I could do anything I liked doing. I'm not the type of person who thinks of the consequences beforehand."

The 'consequences' for Linda would be a revelation. In the studio, McCartney dropped the persona of loving husband and father and Linda found herself suddenly face to face with a stern musical taskmaster. "He had me singing on *Ram* and he'd be like 'Come on! Get it together!' It was nerve wracking because I wasn't a good student so why would I be a good in tune singer," she recalled in the *San Diego Union Tribune*. "He'd get me in tune but I found it hard."

Ram, upon its release in 1971 would be considered an improvement over *McCartney* but it was still an album that, while selling well around the world, was considered by many critics to be tentative and lacking in energy. Linda's efforts were almost grudgingly positive and the only real controversy proved to be McCartney's publishing company raising a raucous about Linda's song royalty rights.

But by that time McCartney and Linda had more concern than another legal issue. On September 13, 1971, Linda gave birth to a third daughter named Stella. It had been a difficult pregnancy that ultimately resulted in a cesarean section birth. Linda was immediately on the mend and was soon back in mother role but, by this time, she had become accustomed to the job description she had taken on as the wife of a Beatle and had evolved, philosophically, to the life task at hand and the idea of being her own person.

"When you find a mate, you just can't go in your own direction," she offered in an *Oobu Joobu.com* radio show interview. "You have to compromise. I was pretty much there when I met Paul. I was a photographer, a lover of life and I was making enough money to support myself. I am still that same person." But in the same interview, Linda was adamant in saying that dealing with a husband is often like dealing with a child. "I think all men are total babies, even when they grow up. Men need mothering. Sometimes when it comes to Paul, I just want to say 'Get on with it kid.' My down to earthness complements his ambition and talent."

And it would not be long after the birth of Stella that Linda once again had to deal with the very thing about McCartney that was always a challenge. The degree of acceptance of his first two post Beatle albums had put the bug in McCartney to once again perform live. Probably the last thing Linda expected, even after her minor contributions to *McCartney* and *Ram*, was that McCartney would ask his wife to join him in a band. But in the world of the McCartneys, it all seemed to make sense. McCartney wanted to play live again but he wanted to be with his family. Linda wanted to be with her husband and children.

Linda would recall in the book *Yesterday: The Unauthorized Biography of Paul McCartney* that her husband sealed the deal by appealing to her sense of ego. "He said to me 'Can you imagine standing on the stage, the curtain going up, the audience all waiting?' He made it sound so glamorous that I agreed to have a go."

So in the end, it all seemed to make sense that Linda should join her husband in Wings. Wings was literally starting from scratch. The other band members were seasoned and capable and it showed in the band's first studio album *Wild Life* which was released to the requisite mixed reviews, decent sales and the expected shots at McCartney for having Linda in the band. Linda took those shots in stride, offering in a 1989 interview with the *San Diego Union Tribune* that attacks on her and McCartney "were just show biz." But Linda acknowledged in that same interview that when McCartney conceived a '*Wings University Tour*' in 1972 as part of their official live coming out, she did experience a bit of stage fright. "I cried before that first show. I was so nervous."

Linda got over her fears during that first tour, acquainting herself quite well on keyboards and harmonies. Low key was the watchword and in keeping with McCartney's sense of simplicity and family values. The two-month tour was set up to allow the band members' families to come along and while juggling motherhood and rock stardom had its moments, Linda's naturalistic approach to life made it all work. "It's quite normal, even on tour with Wings because my feeling has always been what is normal?" she offered in a 1989 interview with the *San Diego Union Tribune*. "I think normal is just not getting on the treadmill of opinions and keeping up with the Joneses. You can be normal anywhere really."

Over the next decade, Linda, who would give birth to a fourth child named James in 1977, witnessed her husband's steady climb from ex-Beatle to superstar in his own right on the strength of hit records and massive tours.

Linda would also look back on the 70's as an era of personal creative growth. Wing's first album, *Wild Life*, would feature a Linda photograph as the album cover. Beginning with their very first tour, Linda, camera in hand, would be everywhere, documenting the band's personal and professional moments. Linda's photography would once again grace the cover of the band's *Red Rose Speedway* album in 1973 and the following year, Linda would make photographic history of a kind when Linda and McCartney, appeared together on the cover of *Rolling Stone* which marked the first time in the history of the magazine that the photographer of the magazine cover also appeared in the photo. By 1975, Linda was the de facto photographer for anything Wings and McCartney, as witness her photo cover for the album *Venus and Mars*.

While seemingly continuing on the minimalist style that highlighted her early work, the subtlety, often extremely basic and simplistic to many observers, was now catching on and admired in many professional circles. McCartney, in conversation with *The Daily Mail*, cut to the quick of his wife's creative skills when he said, "Linda just knew when to click."

Linda, in comments taken from her *Linda McCartney website*, put her style in what she conceived of as a naturalistic perspective. "As far as knowing when to shoot, I've always relied totally on my instinct. I believe I could feel when there was a good picture. It has to deal with the force of inner attention. I think you just feel instinctively. You've got to just click on the moment, not before it and not after it. I think if you're worried about light meters and all that stuff you just miss it."

Linda's gradual ascension to the level of photographer as artist would take a giant step forward in 1976 with the publication of her first book of photos, 'Linda's Pictures: A Collection of Photographs, a collection of early work photographing rock musicians that played up the at large notion that Linda had a natural gift and a great eye for the moment. A year later, Linda's first solo photographic exhibition would hold court at the Jan Baum & Iris Silverman Gallery in Los Angeles. Through 1981, when Wings would officially disband, she photographed the album covers *London Town* and *Back to the Egg*.

During this period, Linda's long held a belief in animal rights and, by association, the lifestyle of vegetarianism came to the fore. In the confines of her relationship with McCartney she had slowly but surely influenced him into a vegetarian lifestyle that had also extended to their children. By the mid 70's, Linda had morphed into a very public and vocal proponent against the concept of animals being killed for food and had become a standard bearer and supporter of such groups as People for the Ethical Treatment of Animals, Friends of the Earth and Council for the Protection of Rural England.

In the website *Brainy Quotes.com* she stated emphatically, "I do not eat anything with a face. If slaughterhouses had glass walls, everybody would be a vegetarian." She was equally in the public's face in *Reading Eagle.com* when she said "Have you ever seen a fish gasping for breath when you take it out of water? It's saying 'Thanks a lot for killing me.'"

Throughout the 70's Linda's questionable talents when it came to music remained as part of the aftermath of the legal battle with McCartney sharing songwriting credits with Linda on the *Ram* album. It was stated in legal proceedings that Linda was not capable of writing songs, which hit Linda particularly hard.

While on a family holiday in 1971, McCartney, as recalled by Linda in *Rolling Stone*, would issue a loving challenge to his wife. "When ATV was suing us, saying that I was incapable of writing, Paul said, 'Get out and write a song.'" Linda took up the challenge and penned a bouncy little Reggae ditty entitled *Seaside Woman*. Linda and McCartney would collaborate on what would be the B side of a proposed single entitled *B Side to Seaside* and, after some years of fits and starts, a single under the pseudonym of Suzy and The Red Stripes, was released in 1977 and had respectable chart success in the US and the UK.

Following the disbanding of Wings, Linda embarked on the decade of the 80's, easily the most productive and creatively satisfying years of her life. Nineteen eight-two saw her shooting the cover for McCartney's album *Tug of War* and the single sleeve photo for Michael Jackson's song *This Girl Is Mine* before bouncing back to familial territory shooting the cover for McCartney's 1983 album *Pipes of Peace*. Nineteen eighty-seven would prove a career highpoint as the first major exhibition of her photos, *Linda McCartney*, went on display at the Royal Photographic Society in Bath, England.

But with the encouragement of McCartney, Linda was always faced with the allure of music and the enticement of playing keyboards. Throughout the mid 80's, Linda attempted formal lessons but had little progress until she contacted former Mott the Hoople and Dexi's Midnight Riders' keyboard player Mick Bolton who offered to teach her a thing or two. In an excerpt from his official bio published in *Ultimate Classic*

Rock, Bolton recalled "Linda had tried various teachers but had found them a bit too serious. What she really wanted was just someone to help her to gain a bit of confidence on the keyboard and to encourage her to enjoy playing. I seemed to be just what she was looking for. I would go down to the farm in Sussex a couple of times a month and we would sit at two keyboards bashing out old rock and roll songs. Linda was never going to be a great keyboard player but she had real enthusiasm for playing and singing."

Linda would make her mark as a truly artistic force in 1988 when she began experimenting with 19th century photographic techniques entitled Sun Prints that would have their official unveiling at the prestigious Victoria & Albert Museum in London. She would return to her pioneering vegetarian campaign with the publication of two cookbooks, *Linda McCartney's Home Cooking* and *Light Lunches*. By 1991, Linda's penchant for all things vegetarian and natural would reach the masses with the launch of her own brand of vegetarian foods, Linda McCartney Foods that would be a financial success, making Linda a now independently wealthy woman in her own right.

Well into the 90's, Linda's creative output would continue at a nonstop pace. A photo book entitled *Sixties: Portrait of an Era* chronicled her rock n'roll photos while a third cookbook, *Main Courses* continued to expand her vegetarian brand.

Linda was cresting the wave of a fairy tale life well into the 90's. She had arrived as her own woman and had managed to leave the stigma of past Beatle wives in the dust. She was fulfilled as a wife, mother and creative entity. If the story ended here, it would be a happy ending.

In December 1995, a malignant tumor was discovered in Linda's breast. "I wasn't feeling well, so I went to a local doctor," she chronicled in an interview with *Linda McCartney: A Biography* author Fields. "He told me I had some kind of cold and to take some pills and wait two weeks. Two weeks later and I still didn't feel better. So we went to London and they tested it and it's cancer. They'll take out the lump and we'll see."

What doctors found was that the cancer had spread to Linda's lymph nodes well before the initial discovery. Linda and McCartney largely pulled back from the public eye as the days, weeks and months ticked away. The couple would be aggressive in fighting Linda's sickness, consulting with doctors in New York, Los Angeles and London, relying primarily on traditional treatments as well as some holistic therapies. In their minds, if there was even a remote chance something might work, they would take the chance.

McCartney would recall in a very candid interview with *USA Weekend* that "We just embarked on a two and a half year program of trying everything we possibly could to turn it around."

Only a small group of intimate family and friends knew of Linda's illness. The last thing Linda wanted was to have what might be her last days turn into a media circus. In that vein, Linda would be scrupulous in making appearances at public events, not wanting to call attention or speculation by her appearance as the cancer slowly but surely progressed. She would be conspicuously absent in the 1996 exhibition of her photography entitled *Roadworks* and did very little to publicize the publication of two new cookbooks, *Linda's Summer Kitchen* and *Linda's Winter Kitchen*.

Through her first round of treatments, those privy to the severity of Linda's cancer would marvel at the fact that her always positive and up attitude resulted in her not acting like a sick person as McCartney reflected in *USA Weekend*. "She never lost her appetite and you're supposed to lose on these things. But Linda was sort of just a lusty person. She'd be like "Right, what are we having for dinner' People around her would be dropping and she'd be saying 'No, don't worry, we're going to lick this thing.'"

Sadly, the cancer had spread and as the final days counted down, Linda and McCartney went to their family ranch in Tucson, Arizona where Linda could spend her final days in the natural world she so loved and where, two days before her death, Linda and McCartney rode horses in the desert one last time. "The horror of her life was that she couldn't ride," McCartney said in *USA Weekend*. "Thank God she was able to ride one last time."

With McCartney at her side, Linda slipped into a coma on the morning of April 17, 1998 and quietly passed at the age of 56. McCartney would take her passing badly, going into a shell to mourn with his children in private. Eventually, he would begin to speak about the death of the love of his life.

"I think I cried for about a year on and off," he told the *BBC*. "You expect to see them walk in, this person you love because you are so used to them. I cried a lot. It seemed like the only thing to do."

Once the crying stopped, McCartney was front and center in continuing to let her memory live on. An album of heretofore unheard Linda composed songs was released and McCartney and their children made themselves available at every opportunity to further animal rights and the lifestyle of vegetarianism. And once he was emotionally ready, he began to speak of his feelings for his lost love.

"It suddenly came to me at the moment she was about to die," he revealed in *USA Weekend*. "I have no idea why, but I just thought 'I've just got to say this to her before she died. You're up on your beautiful Appaloosa stallion, it's a fine Spring day, we're riding through the woods. The bluebells are all out and the sky is clear blue. Those were the last words I said to her…

"And she just drifted off."

Chapter Five
Barbara Bach/Starkey

Unless you've been a diehard fan of all things Beatles, the mention of Barbara Bach would most likely bring a figurative scratch of the head, shrug of the shoulders and a quizzical 'who's that?' Which, in hindsight, is not fair. Bach, in her own low key, below the radar life has been very out there for years, first as the darling of Italian cinema, a top model and part of the reigning attitude of female sex symbols that were very much a part of our culture during the 60's and 70's.

The Spy Who Loved Me producer Cubby Broccoli could not have said it better when he was quoted in *Barbara-Bach.com* as saying "I think that I have been looking all my life for a leading lady who looks like Barbara Bach." Producer director Tony Richardson, on the occasion of screen testing the actress, acknowledged in the same website piece that "Barbara had the look of a tiger. She was tall and streamlined. She was very sexy."

Barbara, in *Weekend Magazine*, was quick to deny that she was all that. "I never felt that I was a fantastic beauty and I did not want to be known as a sex symbol."

Still not quite sure who Barbara Bach is and what she's all about?

Quite simply, Barbara Bach is truly notable for two things. And if you've spent even a modicum of time in the pop culture universe, you're aware of both.

She was a 'Bond girl' named Anya Amasova in the 1977 James Bond epic *The Spy Who Loved Me*. But perhaps most importantly, Barbara Bach was and is the second wife of Beatle Ringo Starr. What is equally tantalizing about this woman who seems to run contrary to Beatle wives' persona is, rather than capitalizing on an already sterling career by being married to a Beatle, Barbara quite simply chose to quit the business.

"I had decided that I did not want to go back to full time working," she told *Weekend Magazine*. "No work had been offered to me that was worth two or three months' separation from my family."

A clue to the fact that Barbara has always seemed worldly and sophisticated in a subtle sort of way can be found in the fact that her parents' roots were wildly international. Her father Howard Irwin Goldbach was Austrian/Jewish, her mother Marjorie Irish/Catholic and, for good measure, Barbara had a grandmother who was Romanian.

Howard Goldbach was recently retired from the military and Marjorie lived a fairly satisfying and frugal life according to an article in *Queens Chronicle*. At the time of Bach's birth on August 27, 1947, the family, with Howard then serving as a New York City police officer, was living in a veteran's funded housing tract in East Elmhurst. When the housing tract was defunded in 1952, the now growing Goldbach family, which already included an older brother and, after Barbara, would include a younger brother and sister, moved to a house in Rosedale, a suburb of Queens.

What little is known of Barbara's early years is scattered at best. What is known is that although her father was Jewish, the children were all raised in the Roman Catholic faith, with Barbara attending an all-girls convent school called Dominican Commercial High School, where she sang in the girls glee club, played basketball and, into her teens, was a huge music fan of the likes of Aretha Franklin and The Rolling Stones. Michael Seth Starr, author of the biography *Ringo Starr: With a Little Help*, acknowledged in an interview with the author that, "As far as I know, she had a fairly typical upbringing."

An upbringing that, at age 15, saw Barbara having a very prophetic encounter with The Beatles when, in 1965, she acted as chaperone for her younger sister Marjorie at The Beatles Shea Stadium concert with 50,000 screaming Beatle fans. Years later, Barbara would recall to *People* that she may well have been the only teenager who was not thrilled to be there. "I wasn't exactly a raging Beatlemaniac. I liked Bob Dylan, Ray Charles and The Rolling Stones. But I kind of had to go to keep an eye on my sister."

By the time Barbara had turned 16, she had evolved into quite the attractive girl, with a look that exuded style and grace and could come across as any number of ethnicities, alternately appearing very American or very European. It also did not hurt that she had also become fairly fluent in several languages. She had modeling in her DNA and, after having the idea turn into a dream, Barbara left school in 1964 to become a model. That same year, Barbara signed with the famed Eileen Ford Modeling Agenc*y* when she made another decision.

Goldbach was her name but it was not a 'model' type name and so she decided to shorten her name to Bach.

Barbara's entry into the modeling scene coincided with the rise of the 'It' girl image of the moment in fashion and, by association, modeling. She seemed to have exactly what pop culture and society were looking for at the time and, almost immediately, her face and her body became an in demand commodity. She graduated from catalogue assignments to a breakthrough photo session for the magazine *Seventeen* which catapulted her to the ranks of top models in the space of a year by the time she reached the age of 18. Barbara was now the most sought after and one of the highest paid models in the business, landing on the covers of such magazines as *Elle*, *Vogue* and, on several occasions, *Seventeen.*

Assignments would often find Barbara jetting off to far flung international cities and so it was in 1966 when, on a flight to Rome, she made the acquaintance of a fellow passenger, a much older Italian businessman, by 11 years, named Augusto Gregorini. In an extensive biography *Barbara-Bach.com*, Barbara recalled the moment they met and how it was love at first sight.

"I first went to Italy on a modeling assignment. I met this attractive Italian on the plane and he eventually convinced me that it would be much nicer living in Italy for my career. I rang up my parents and told them that I would be moving to Italy. My parents were not thrilled with the idea but they eventually got used to it."

Within months of relocating to Rome, Barbara and Gregorini were married. Besides love and marriage, Barbara soon discovered that her now husband was right in saying her modeling career would take off in Italy with her image soon gracing such noted Italian publications as *Giola*, *Amica* and *Bella* as well as other international publications that included *Elle* (France), *Monique* (Canada), *New Mode* (Germany), *Figurino* (Brazil) and *Diez Minutos* (Spain).

Barbara's ability to adjust to new people and places had made the adjustment to living in Italy an easy transition as she related in *Barbara-Bach.com*. "I adore Italy. After a year I became fluent in the language and stopped feeling foreign. But the natives would constantly remind me that I was American."

Barbara was walking down the street one day, not long after relocating to Italy when she was approached by a man who made her an offer she could not refuse. "He asked me if I would do something for television," she recalled to *Weekend Magazine*. "I had done TV commercials so I knew the difference between appearing for a still camera and one used for motion pictures. It was one of those things that they say happens and it did."

The result of this encounter was that Barbara would make her acting debut in 1967 in the television series *Cordialmente*. Gregorini was outwardly happy for Barbara's first big acting break but it was reported that he was a man known for loving anonymity and so was a bit uncomfortable with his wife always being in the public eye. But he loved his wife and would not be one to stand in her way.

Barbara's continued climb in the film world would grow in 1968 when she landed a small role in the Italian television mini-series *The Odyssey*. It was significant that while she was filming *The Odyssey*, Barbara was several months pregnant. The couples' first child, a daughter named Francesca, was born later that year. By all accounts, Barbara adapted well to motherhood but it soon became evident that her career was of equal importance. Not long after Francesca was born Barbara continued to be the darling of the modeling world and her face and figure would continue to grace magazine covers all over the world.

Good notices from her work in *The Odyssey* would also result in offers for film roles. Despite almost nonexistent acting education, Barbara brought a lot to the roles when it came to Italian cinema. While she did not speak Italian with an accent, the speech patterns she had acquired while living in Italy did sound foreign. That she was bilingual in English and Italian was a plus. Barbara did four films in 1971, *Black Belly of the Tarantula*, *Mio Padre Monsignore*, *Short Night of Glass Dolls* and *A Few Hours* and proved quite capable in the genres of comedy, romance and thriller in support roles. "I spoke Italian in my first movies," she said in *Barbara-Bach.com*. "The only time they had to dub my voice was in a French movie."

By the end of the year, Barbara was once again pregnant and gave birth to a son named Gianni Andrea in 1972. Barbara's film career would continue to flourish. There were plenty of parts for her but most were essentially ciphers, playing predictable types with little room to creatively grow in what had evolved into an endless stream of B movie horror and suspense films. If Barbara was troubled by the endless array of predictable parts, she was not complaining. Point of fact, nobody she had ever worked with thought of her as anything but a consummate professional on a movie set. But while her professional life was flourishing, her marriage was slowly grinding to a dead end.

Barbara and Gregorini would separate in 1975. She would leave Italy and relocate to Los Angeles with the children. As celebrity divorces often do, it would take another three years, into 1978, before their divorce was final. Barbara looked back wistfully at the disillusion of her first marriage in *Barbara-Bach.com*. "My husband and I were more friends than anything else. And we still are. What happened to our marriage? Our lives took different paths. But there's no recrimination."

Nor did she think the 12 years she spent with Gregorini were a waste of time. "My marriage was by no means a mistake," she told *People*. "I have two wonderful kids and I learned a whole new culture. It just wasn't a lifetime commitment."

But the experience did plant in Barbara a newfound, feminist attitude toward the concept of marriage that seemed quite in line with women's rising sense of liberation at that period in her life. In a 1981 interview with *Playboy*, she would look back on those days of coming to terms with being an independent woman.

"I can't imagine I would ever get married again," she said at that time. "I made that commitment once and was unable to fulfill it. The way I am now, if I want to be with someone, I'll be with that person. But I see no reason to carry his name as well. I'm still me and I've worked hard to achieve that much for someone who has been married and has two wonderful children. Marriage would make no sense."

Resuming her career in Los Angeles, Barbara once again found herself in demand for yet another round of 'spaghetti horror' films like *Island of the Fishmen* and *The Humanoid and the Unseen*. It was on the latter film that she entered her first post divorce relationship with cinematographer Roberto Quezada. She was a working actress in a B movie world but she continued being the consummate professional. "I always wanted to do things that I was proud of and work with people I admire," she was quoted in a *Sentstarr.com* biography. "That's the kind of drive I had."

And it was a drive that eventually brought her to the attention of producer Cubby Broccoli who was casting around for the female lead in his latest James Bond epic *The Spy Who Loved Me*. He liked her look, the high cheekbones, the face and figure. And after viewing footage of nine of Barbara's previous Italian films, he could see that she was a capable actress who, in line with the long-standing Bond credo of hiring talented unknowns who would work cheap, checked all the right boxes. The next step was a short notice call and a screen test with Broccoli and the film's director Lewis Gilbert.

Barbara would recall in *Barbara-Bach.com* that, "I did the test on a Tuesday. They saw it on a Wednesday and I got a call from Mr. Broccoli inviting me to lunch with him and Mr. Gilbert. I did not know if I had gotten the part. I didn't have the courage to ask. Then at lunch they told me I had the part. I was so excited that I couldn't eat anything."

The Spy Who Loved Me opened with all the expected Hollywood glitz and glamour and Barbara was swept along for the ride. As the latest in what had already become an international following for Bond Girls and, in her very first English language film role, she became a critical success with many citing her role as Anya as one of the most truly realized roles in the history of the Bond franchise. A year later Barbara would show her action film chops as a down and dirty freedom fighter in *Force Ten from Navarone.*

It was in 1979 that Barbara was offered the role of a lifetime. Kate Jackson had just left the television series *Charlie's Angeles*. Barbara, as reported in *The New York Daily News*, *The Johnny Carson Show* and countless other outlets, seemed the perfect choice for the series but was ultimately rejected on the grounds that she came across as too sophisticated and not American enough (despite the fact that she was born in Queens, New York.) Barbara would couch the rejection in humor and irony in a conversation with *Playboy.* "The producers thought I was too European and too sophisticated. I didn't take them seriously enough when they asked questions like 'What sports do you play and what brought you to Hollywood?' In the end, I sensed it was not whether I could act but whether I could bounce."

Still, Barbara had wanted the part and was visibly disappointed at the rejection. But she would salve her disappointment by returning to Italy where she continued to model and returned to her B movie roots with starring roles in the movies *Jaguar Lives* and *The Great Alligator.*

But life took an unexpected turn in 1980 when Barbara was offered a big part in a prehistoric comedy called *Caveman* which starred Ringo Starr. *Caveman* was very low-grade slapstick in conception and the buzz on the movie even before filming began was not good. But to be perfectly candid, Starr had seemingly had no choice but to say yes.

His post Beatles career was in decline with solo albums, after a promising start, not doing well. His impending divorce from first wife Maureen was turning nasty. He was keeping time with a girlfriend, Nancy Andrews, who had been the last straw in his marriage and was, in hindsight, looking shaky at best. Throw in a growing alcohol and drug problem and Barbara's co-star was the poster boy for Hollywood mess.

But, according to author Michael Seth Starr, Barbara had most certainly crossed paths with this type before. "When she met Ringo on the set of *Caveman*, Barbara had already been around celebrities for years as both a model and as an actress. So, I imagine she was well aware of the pressures faced by stars of Ringo's magnitude and the celebrity environment that often creates those pressures."

On the set of *Caveman*, Barbara would prove the proverbial trooper, throwing herself, sometimes literally, into every scene, being congenial with other cast members and was quick with the compliments when the press came around, especially when it came to her co-star. "Ringo is so interesting, a really nice guy," she gushed to *Playboy*. "I think Richard's going to be marvelous in this picture."

Although the relationship between Barbara and Starr appeared professional and aboveboard when filming, there were signs that the relationship off camera was beginning to smolder. The press got wind of what was going on and were quick to print reports of an on-set romance. And more than one crew member would acknowledge, anonymously, that the pair were often spotted walking together on the set, were holding hands and gazing lovingly into each other's eyes.

It sure looked like love at first sight but Barbara would tell *Playboy* that nothing could be further from the truth. "The truth is we weren't together until the very end of *Caveman*. Working we got along fine but we each had other people in our lives. Then all of a sudden within a week, the last week of shooting, it just happened. We changed from friendly love to being in love. It wasn't quite love at first sight but it began to grow within minutes of meeting each other."

The couple would cement the seriousness of their budding relationship shortly after the completion of *Caveman* when Ringo invited her to his home in Monte Carlo to witness the Monaco Grand Prix. The couple would look back on those early days with growing fondness.

Barbara referred to Starr as quiet, sensitive and intelligent while Starr was equally smitten when he described Barbara as beautiful, sexy, funny and warm hearted. Ultimately it would take a near death experience to unite the two lovers forever.

On May 19, 1980, Barbara and Starr were driving to a party when they suddenly drove into a fog bank and right into the path of an oncoming truck. Their car was travelling at 60 mph when Starr, attempting to avoid the truck, went into a skid that had the car go into a somersaulting skid that ended with their car smashing head on into a pair of lampposts. As it was reported in the worldwide press, Starr, sustained a leg injury in the crash, reached into the wreckage and pulled Barbara out. They were taken to a nearby hospital with what would turn out to be only minor injuries. But the incident would bond the couple in a way that only a near death experience could produce.

Almost immediately, they pledged their never-ending commitment to each other. Barbara was particularly bonded to Starr at that moment. Three weeks after the accident, Barbara rang up her father and told him, in no uncertain terms, that she was going to marry Starr. A marriage announcement would be forthcoming in July of that year with the ceremony scheduled for April 27 1981.

The marriage was typical of what Beatle nuptials had been to that point, largely low key by design and ultimately mild chaos as the event was conveniently released to the press. In the case of Barbara and Starr, a very simple ceremony was held at Marylebone Register Office in London. The wedding party was limited to 15 family members and friends but as it turned out an estimated 350 screaming fans had also made their way to the wedding office and were adding a nostalgic touch of Beatlemania to the proceedings. But what made the gathering enticing was the fact that George Harrison and Paul McCartney and their wives were in attendance. Which only added to the excitement and speculation of what this mini-reunion of The Beatles might produce. Following the ceremony, Barbara, Starr and the wedding party went to an exclusive club called *Rags* for the wedding reception where it turned out somebody had delivered three guitars for the occasion, hoping against hope that a mini-Beatle jam session might take place. It did not.

Barbara and Starr were now officially man and wife and, by all reports, those first few months were wedded bliss. But bubbling beneath the surface were some demons ready to strike.

After some initial success in his post Beatles' career, Starr's cachet was on the decline. Being a former Beatle did not guarantee stardom in the case of Starr, with subsequent albums in the early 80's being dismal commercial failures. Not long after Barbara and Starr said their ' I do's, the drummer found himself without a record label for the first time in his professional career. His attempts at acting had produced much notoriety and little box office and it was considered a sign of Starr's creative downturn that he had accepted the role in *Caveman* because it was the only offer at the time.

For her part, Barbara, largely by design, had, with marriage, retreated from the public eye, more interested in being a wife and mother than working. The work she would contribute to over the next decade would be negligible at best, an appearance in a short entitled *The Cooler* (1982), a little seen or noticed television mini-series called *Princess Daisy* (1983) and a miniscule moment in the film adaptation of McCartney's *Give My Regards to Broadstreet* (1984).

It was no small coincidence that Starr also had roles in all three films because Barbara and Starr were conspicuous by the fact that they were now literally joined at the hip if they did go out. Which given their slow but progressing addiction to drugs and alcohol was rare. Although there had always been reports of Barbara being a bit of a hard party type, Starr, in a conversation with *People*, took full responsibility for bringing her into a hard drinking/hard drugging life.

"Barbara fell into the trap because of me. She was an actress who used to go to bed at 10:00 and get up at 8:00 in the morning. Until we met. Then her career went the same way as mine."

The decade of the 80's saw the couple in deep decline. A drug and alcohol routine, which reportedly included daily cocaine use by Barbara, often found Barbara and Starr sitting in front of the television for days on end, drinking and drugging themselves into oblivion. One of those who remembered those dark days was Barbara's daughter Francesca who told *The Sun* that the best thing that happened to her was that she was sent away to boarding school. "Their troubles made me a better academic. When I was living with them I was always hidden in my room reading because Mum and Dad were always out of it."

Holding nothing back in later years, Barbara and Starr would recall, in a forward to the book *Getting Sober* by Derrick Taylor, just how bad things would get. "We used to go on long plane journeys, rent huge villas, stock up the bars, hide and get deranged."

101

In her more lucent moments, Barbara would, as recalled by Starr in *People*, attempt to pull the couple out of their doomed spiral. "Every couple of months, Barbara would try and straighten us out but then we'd fall right back into the trap."

A trap that, by this time, had become painfully public according to an *InsideEdition.com* quote from *Ringo With a Little Help* author Michael Stef Starr. "They had lots of arguments in public. At the time, Barbara was smart enough to realize that this had to stop or they would die." But despite Barbara's continued efforts, their addiction only got worse.

Barbara would appear in her final motion picture acting role in 1986 as part of an elephant polo playing team in the comedy *To the North of Katmandu*. As with her previous films of the mid to late 80's, Starr would also have a small role. To the public, it seemed an amusing bit of business. To those who knew the couple's addictive situation, it seemed kind of pathetic, a once mighty power couple snapping at crumbs in order to stay relevant.

Barbara and Starr would continue in this downward spiral well into the late 80's. Starr, who had a reputation of getting blind drunk and not remembering what and where he had been the night before would dramatically bring their situation to a head as he would confess in a story from the book *Still The Greatest* by Andrew Grant Jackson. "It was 1988 and I had came to one Friday afternoon in our house. I was told by the house staff that I had trashed the house so badly that they thought there had been burglars and that I had trashed Barbara so bad that they thought she was dead."

While not physically harmed, Barbara would confess to *People* that the incident was a breaking point for her. "I got used to living at the bottom but you get to the point when you realize that this isn't living."

In the aftermath of Starr's violent episode, the couple assessed what their lives had become. "We desperately needed to change," she told *People*. Starr's response, as he offered in *Parade* was "I said to Barbara 'you've got to get us into one of those rehab places. She called some friends of ours who knew where we should go."

The couple entered Sierra Tucson Rehab Clinic that same year. They both finally realized they had a problem that needed to be dealt with. Barbara put it quite succinctly when she told *People* "We went into rehab because we needed desperately to change." And they went together, sharing a room at the clinic while they spent six weeks turning their lives around.

The following year Starr formed the Ringo Starr All Star Band which, equal parts therapy and attempt to revitalize his career, brought him out of his turmoil. Collectively, Barbara and Starr would gravitate toward a more peaceful lifestyle that included meditation and vegetarianism. For her part, Barbara would rekindle her passion for riding horses and charity work, adding her celebrity cachet to a number of charities related to helping orphans and, with Starr, being spokespersons for alcoholism-related organizations. And in 1993, Barbara redirected her energies toward education by getting a Masters Degree in Psychology at UCLA.

But perhaps the most fitting epilogue to Barbara Bach's life as a Beatle wife is that, going into 2021, the now 74 year-old Bach and her 80 year-old ex Beatle have remained inseparable through all the ups and downs and, yes it is cliché, that the old axiom holds true.

Love does conquer all.

Chapter Six
Yoko Ono Lennon

Did Yoko Ono break up The Beatles? That is the question.

In all fairness to Yoko, she may well have helped in the band's demise but the reality was that The Beatles were going off the rails long before she arrived on the scene. If there was a culprit, the numerous lawyers, financial battles and the slow but sure disintegration of good friendships all had a hand in it. But, at the end of the day, blaming all those elements was a lot of hard work for those who lived and breathed everything about The Beatles and more work than they were willing to stomach.

Blaming Yoko for the breakup took a lot less work.

And in all honesty, Yoko was partially at fault. She was, from the get go, an often not too subtle manipulator and con artist of John Lennon. She has always had her agendas, be they creative, emotional, social or political and, in hindsight, she found the perfect tool in John Lennon. For all his ego-driven bluster and rebellious nature, Lennon, at his emotional core, had, by the time Yoko was on the scene, evolved into a sensitive, emotionally scattered and insecure man who was, for better or worse, susceptible to Yoko's prodding and subtle suggestions that he go and do certain things. But does all of that make Yoko a conniving and controlling bitch?

Yoko, now into her late 80's and in declining health, has had negativity heaped on her for literally decades. But she has remained defiant in the face of the charges that she single handedly brought down the most dominating musical force in history. She's been upfront in defending herself and, depending on her mood, has been alternately straightforward, philosophical and sometimes whimsical in deflecting the charges.

"I had nothing to do with breaking up The Beatles," she emphatically told *US Weekly*. She was in full on defensive posture when she told *AZQuotes.com* "I did not break up The Beatles. If you're going to blame me for breaking up The Beatles, you should be thankful that I made them into a myth rather than a crumbling group." She did admit to *The Daily Mail Online* that being the target of what she perceived as lies was not easy to take. "For many years I was hated by the whole world. I was painted as a dragon. I had to deal with that. I could have turned and ran. But that was never an option." Another *Daily Mail Online* quote showed her expressing the humor and irony of it all. "I did not break up The Beatles. My small hands could not have broken those men up."

And as she would ruefully relate in a conversation with *Interview*, it is a preconception that, even to this day, will not go away. "People tend to address me first as the wife of John, then the widow of John and finally the person who broke up The Beatles."

The life of Yoko began years and, most likely, countless decades before her birth, at a time when wealth, position and a dynastic sense of aristocracy were the world in which her parents, father Eisuke and mother Isoko had lived and thrived. Almost from birth, the couple became part and parcel of the upper class where political and social connections were valued above all else and bankers were the ones who influenced and affected Japan and its history.

Yoko would take notice of how her parents and, most importantly, the Yasuda dynasty, who came from a decades old family of Samurai warriors and scholars, were responsible for the rise of financial power and importance in an interview with *BriefAndToThePoint.com*.

"My great, great grandfather, Yasuda, the creator of the family's wealth, was the son of a Samurai. My great grandfather, Zenjiro, created a huge financial power. In those days, bankers were the people who were seriously changing the world. In a historical sense, it made Eisuke the odd man out in the family. He was creatively inclined and sensitive who, from an early age, was pointing toward a career as a concert pianist."

"But my father, who was a concert pianist, had a different view," she recalled in *BriefAndToThePoint.com*. "He said 'no they [bankers] are not the ones. It's going to be music that's going to change the world.'"

Years later and in interviews with *National Public Radio* and *BestClassicBands.com*, there was real emotion as she remembered what her father could have been. "My father was a banker but he was an independent spirit. He was a very good pianist and very much into music. My father always wanted to be a pianist. He went to the point of doing concerts and getting good reviews. But his father wanted him to inherit the family business so he went that way."

Isoko was also quite accomplished in the creative world. She was quite the notable painter for her time and was quite fluent in the art of Japanese music and instrumentation.

Being an international banker meant lots of travel and periods of time in different parts of the world which meant that by the time Eisuke and Isoko married, his banking duties would keep the couple apart for long periods of time.

And so it was with highly mixed emotions that, when Yoko Ono was born in the splendor of Kamakuro, Japan on February 18, 1933, Eisuke was thousands of miles away in San Francisco seeing to a large aspect of the growing Japanese empire. Left primarily in the hands of house servants and the inconsistent attention of a mother who was often more interested in narcissistic pursuits, the first two years of Yoko's life flew by in a flash of privilege and isolation. Isoko could be candid to the point of being hurtful in the assessment of her daughter, as evidenced, according to Yoko's comments in *Vulture.com* in which she recalled the time her mother called her "handsome but not pretty."

In 1935, Isoko and Yoko would go to San Francisco to reunite with Eisuke. Even at the age of two, Yoko would recall in a *National Public Radio* interview that the moment she met her father for the first time was not lost on the young child. "It was a big moment. And the time that I met him, my mother and father were kissing and I was like 'maybe he is going to kiss me too.'"

Yoko's parents were both work oriented and self-absorbed and it was at these early stages of development that Yoko was often ignored and isolated. So much so that Yoko would often just ring for the maid just so she would have another person to connect with. But what Eisuke and Isoko lacked in parenting skills, they more than made up for with a persistent approach to her education and, in particular, her creative side. By age four, Yoko was enrolled in the elite Japanese school Gakushuin where she was exposed to the likes of Bach, Beethoven and Brahms. She would give her first solo piano recital that same year and was, to the amazement of her instructors, already composing mature poetic haikus.

But even at that early age, Yoko had a sense that she was out of step with formal education practices as she offered in *The Japan Times*. "My ideas from the beginning were extremely different. The boundaries that were set up in this society and the proscribed forms of art were something that I ignored from the beginning."

By 1941, the Ono family was once again on the move.

After a short stay in New York, the growing tide of anti-Japanese sentiment with the onset of World War II forced them to return to Japan where, in a wide-ranging attempt to fund the Japanese war movement, all of their wealth was diverted from the family to the Japanese government and the war effort and the once upper class Ono family was suddenly forced to live like peasants. Day to day survival was alien to the privileged Ono family but they were quick to adjust. It was while living among farmers and on a subsistence level that often saw the family selling prized bits of clothing in order to get enough money to buy food. During the fire-bombing of Tokyo in 1945, the family hid in a basement and miraculously survived while houses all around them burned. It was a time of emotional and introspective thinking on the part of Yoko who began to experience the first barbs of racism.

"When I was so young, I did get racism directed toward me," she recalled in conversation with *The Japan Times*. "And it didn't happen just in the US. When I went back to Japan I was kind of delicately ostracized. Just the way I acted, I seemed a bit different from other kids. Also when we were evacuated to the countryside because of the bombing, the farmers would not be happy with city people."

With the end of the war, Yoko would remain in Japan while her family relocated back to New York. She returned to Gakushuin University where she had the distinction of becoming the first woman to be accepted into the school's philosophy program. But the frustration with the educational norm continued to blunt her interest and within a year, she would leave Gakushuin and return to the states to enroll in Sarah Lawrence University.

Yoko's parents would approve because of the arts and creative oriented nature of the school's curriculum. During her three years at Sarah Lawrence, Yoko would avail herself of the school's topflight curriculum and notable instructors. She would learn poetry with Alastair Reid, English Literature with Kathryn Mansell and, perhaps most importantly, music composition with Andre Singer.

Yoko was finding her own way musically, a mixture of progressive and jazz elements that were evolving into a form of the then up and coming style of 12 Tone music, a style big on minimalism and the avant garde.

Singer sensed that Yoko was not thinking in orthodox musical terms and, in a quote from a *GettyRecordingArtists.com* story he told her as much. "You know, your stuff is getting very far out and all that and there's some very experimental people, people like John Cage, in New York who are doing things." Yoko took the hint and, once again struggling against the norms of proper education, dropped out of Sarah Lawrence.

"I was a dropout of Sarah Lawrence," she said in *GettyRecording Artists.com*. "You usually don't drop out after three years. I just thought it was so crazy to stay there because so many exciting things were happening elsewhere."

Yoko's decision to drop out of Sarah Lawrence and live a bohemian lifestyle with creative types they did not approve of was the final nail in the coffin of a parent/child relationship that had resulted from years of neglect and disinterest. In desperation, Yoko's parents wielded what they perceived as the last bit of power they had over their daughter. Yoko, who was now in total rebellion form, sealed the deal in a truly avant garde manner when she sent her parents a bottle filled with urine as a parting gift.

In a conversation with *TheNational.com*, Yoko would, grudgingly, acknowledge that her choice of art had much to do with the falling out with her parents. "I'm sure they wouldn't have minded if I had become a kind of accepted artist or an accepted composer. But I don't think they liked the fact that what I was doing was so rebellious. It was not that I set out to be rebellious. It was just in my nature to be that way."

Yoko was now into a brave new world.

She was enthralled with the lifestyle, meeting with the likes of John Cage, La Monte Young and a seemingly endless number of poets, artists and musicians who were making an artistic stand. Almost immediately, Yoko became a cog in the emerging scene, appearing dressed down in all black with long, scraggly hair at the art happenings and gallery openings and supporting herself in her new lifestyle with a series of low level waitressing, teaching and management jobs

What she was finding was that the creative population of what was being called in the mainstream press as 'Generation Beat' was encouragement to be herself. Yoko began making her way as a performance artist and painter who would often be a part of the show in many performances staged at her Chambers Street loft.

The likes of Cage and Young were quick to 'get' what Yoko was about and would regularly feature her in their own performances. One memorable John Cage performance featured an early Yoko creative moment in which she created an impromptu piece of art and then set it on fire. During her first solo performance in 1961, Yoko debuted the first of what would be many interactive conceptual pieces with *Painting To Be Stepped On.* That same year she performed in a recital hall which featured the amplified sound of a toilet flushing.

Those early performances would highlight Yoko's instinctive and highly improvisational performing style that featured discordant instrumental and vocal styles that often tested the audience's tolerance for just what art was. Yoko would define the early development of her performance art in a *Seattle Times* interview when she offered, "I was not afraid at all of what I did on stage. It was just me and I could do whatever I wanted to do."

But Yoko was smart enough to know that there was a fair amount of sexism, albeit subtle, in even the most progressive movements and, as she related in *The National*, she would fight long and hard to get her opinions and attitudes across. "It was always a battle being a female artist. The avant garde world was not any different from the jazz world. It was very macho."

In 1956, Yoko met Juilliard school student and avant garde pianist Toshi Ichiyanagi. At the same age and born in Japan, the pair instantly found an attraction based on creative interests. It would almost be an afterthought that Toshi and Yoko would fall in love. Breaking the news to Yoko's parents that the couple was engaged did not go well. Yoko's class-conscious parents did not approve of the relationship because Toshi did not come from a wealthy family. In one last act of defiance, Yoko and Toshi eloped and, in short order, were living a freewheeling creative life in a New York loft.

By all accounts, the relationship between the newlyweds was good, evolving as it would their respective creative passions. But the very thing that brought them together would very quickly dissolve all pretense of a marriage through a never ending clashing of creative ideologies and they soon began living apart, although they would remain good friends and work in the same creative circles. When Toshi relocated back to Japan in 1962, Yoko would follow. It was in the next year that Yoko would face her darkest moments. Her attempts to bring her artistic style to a Japanese audience were often met with derision. It was also during that period that the couple would finalize divorce proceedings.

Yoko fell into a deep and dark depression which resulted in a nervous breakdown and a failed suicide attempt overdosing on pills, before being admitted to a mental institution. In a conversation with *The National*, Yoko calmly addressed the suicide. "I was suicidal in my teen years as well. It wasn't just when I came back to Japan. It was always like I felt suicidal."

For his part, Toshi took the breakup with Yoko in both a stoic and sad manner, acknowledging in a long ago letter to John Cage that "I am sorry that I could not make Yoko happy."

Yoko's time in the mental institution is fragmentary at best. The answer to treating her extreme depression was to keep her constantly sedated and in isolation. It is not known if she was allowed any visitors but what is known is that one Anthony Cox, a sometime actor, jazz musician and art scene scenester and promotor did manage to track her down and visit her. In her mentally depressed and sedated state, Yoko was not necessarily in the state of mind to be greeting a male admirer. But Cox, through compliments about her work and how wonderful a person and artist she was, was just the tonic for the mentally scattered Yoko. Through machinations that, to this day remain unclear, Cox managed to get Yoko released from the institution and took her back to New York where, in late 1962, they were married.

But in what had obviously been an impulsive move, Yoko would run afoul of the legal system when the marriage was annulled on March 1, 1963 because she had failed to finalize her first marriage to Toshi. Problem solved, Yoko and Cox would remarry for a second time in June 1963. But by that time, the impulsive rush to the altar was already beginning to show cracks.

Cox was behaving more like a promoter/manager than a husband while Yoko, once again in New York, was feeling a resurgence in creative spirit which led to her plunging back into her old stomping grounds in the New York avant garde scene. The true test of whatever the relationship meant came in early 1963 when Yoko discovered that she was pregnant. A lot of her damaged relationship with her parents once again came rushing back and she told Cox in no uncertain terms that she wanted an abortion. Cox insisted that she have the child and a war of wills ensued. Yoko and Cox struck an unspoken deal in which Cox would be the primary caregiver of the child while continuing to be an active promoter of Yoko's work. In August 1963, Yoko and Cox welcomed a baby girl named Kyoko into the world.

The decade of the 60's was a watershed moment for Yoko. Riding the wave of conceptual and performance art, coupled with an aggressive in your face approach to artistic issues of class, gender and cultural identity, Yoko's progressive attitudes had suddenly landed her as an artistic pioneer whose every art project would take on enormous cultural and artistic importance. Although she is always mentioned as an early exponent with the coming of the influential *Fluxus* art movement, the reality was that she had declined to become an actual member of the group, the better to maintain her all-important independence.

Yoko's creative conceits would be spread out through several media forms. *Cut Piece* (1964) was easily one of her most defiant works, a performance of conceptual art in which Yoko, dressed in a suit and holding scissors in her hand, invites members of the audience to come on stage and snip off a piece of her clothing. There is built in tension and a not too subtle assault on women's rights and cultural norms as audience members gradually become more aggressive in their cutting and Yoko is reduced to near naked and kneeling as her clothes continue to fall away. Nineteen sixty-four was also the year that Yoko made her publishing debut with a chapbook of proposals, prompts and instructions called *Grapefruit*. By the mid 60's, Yoko was spreading her wings in the arena of experimental filmmaking with a continued art house favorite called *Film No. 4 (Bottoms)* in which an endless number of men and woman shake their butts for the camera.

Yoko's approach to art was considered beyond avant-garde for the time and she would, in years to come, give many spirited discourses to the press as to just what she was doing. In an interview with *The Art Newspaper*, Yoko would defend her approach to art as something very much of the moment.

"When I get an idea, I choose the medium or should I say that the idea itself chooses the medium. What kept me going in the past was an arrogant Van Gogh complex. The idea that an artist has to make works that are truly artistic. In those days I never thought that the things I was doing would ever leave a trace afterwards."

In 1966, Yoko was well on her way to avant-garde celebrity. She was being seen in the more prestigious galleries and performance halls and laudatory reviews of her work were now the norm. A sure sign of her growing notoriety was that she was being courted in London, a town and a scene that was undergoing a scene change that fit, creatively and culturally, into what Yoko was about. And so when a very hip and now art gallery called *Indico* requested an exhibition of her work, Yoko was on her way to what she would later tell *Mojo* opened her eyes.

"The whole scene, from the point of view of an American, was very underground, very intimate, very high quality. There was a strange kind of shimmer in the London air and it was beautiful. Once I breathed that, I felt like 'Okay. I'm here.'"

This breath of fresh air was exactly what Yoko needed. Her marriage to Cox was rapidly deteriorating to that of business manager and employee and she would acknowledge in her private moments that she was considering having affairs. Yoko would lay herself emotionally bare in an article on the website *Madelinx.com* with quotes attributed to *Mojo* and a long ago Yoko Tweet.

"In 1966, I was in a totally difficult situation in my life. I was feeling totally alone. I was getting cynical and getting scared and thinking that men were a necessary evil. I was telling myself that I was too busy to think about men."

Given her state of mind, it was no wonder that Yoko was a bit upset when, the day before her exhibit at the *Indico* was set to open, the gallery owner unexpectedly appeared with his good friend John Lennon. "I was a little bit furious," she revealed in *Madelinex.com*. "I told the gallery owner never to bring anybody to the gallery until the exhibit was open to the public. I said 'okay maybe he's a close friend or something.' So I followed them around and paid close attention."

In Lennon, Yoko would later assess a person who was not dealing with worldwide celebrity well. Riding out the last vestiges of Beatlemania and the death throes of the band, Lennon, also faced with the slow but certain dissolution of his first marriage, had gone into an emotional shell, struggling creatively and emotionally with life. But Yoko's first impression of Lennon did not take any of those issues into consideration as she acknowledged in *Uncut: The Ultimate Music Guide*. "The first impression I had of him was that he looked very beautiful, a very elegant kind of guy. There was a nice feeling about it, that it would be nice to have an affair or something with somebody like this."

Yoko's initial impression of Lennon would change as she followed Lennon and the gallery owner around. He was somebody who was alternately condescending, arrogant and more than a bit of a bully. It was obvious that he did not think much of Yoko's art, a bag of nails and an apple seated on a Plexiglas stand brought a torrent of belittling and condescending remarks. But what would instantly draw Yoko's wrath was when Lennon decided to mess with her apple piece.

"He just grabbed it [the apple], had a bite out of it and looked at me like 'there you know,' she told *The Telegraph*. "I was so furious. I didn't know what to say. And it all showed in my face. How dare this person mess around with my work. So he just said 'I'm sorry' and just put the apple back on the stand."

All the good vibes she had about Lennon were immediately replaced by disdain as she continued to follow him around the gallery and up to what Yoko called her 'Yes' painting, a truly conceptual piece in which the viewer ascended a ladder to the ceiling where they were met with a canvas and a magnifying glass on a chain. It was a work of art that was deeply personal as Yoko offered in a *Twitter message* some years later. "When I made the Yes painting in 1966, I was in a totally different situation in my life and I thought what I needed was a Yes and so I put the word on the ceiling."

The irony was that after Lennon ascended the ladder and discovered the word on the canvas, his whole demeanor seemed to change. Yoko's work had struck at something he craved, a certain something that seemed to be absent in his life. The Yes painting had effectively opened up a link between John and Yoko. And they both sensed it.

Over the next 17 months, Yoko would, after a fairly sedate relationship with the high brow avant garde art press, suddenly find herself in the crosshairs of an often predatory/sensationalist media who saw her even passing association with Lennon as a sign to bare their claws. Anything associated even remotely with The Beatles was considered front-page news and though there would be hints of something brewing between Yoko and Lennon, in those early days and months it seemed, to Yoko, to be absurdly overblown and outlandish.

"John and I were just getting together," she told *Uncut Magazine*. "It could happen to anybody. It was just a man and a woman getting together." But years later, Yoko would speculate with *The Telegraph* how she should have seen the handwriting on the wall. "In a way, John and I both ruined our careers by getting together, although we weren't aware of it at the time."

But what Yoko would become quickly aware of was that even the slightest gesture would be ripe for misinterpretation. One of the earliest was that Yoko had sent Lennon a copy of her book *Grapefruit*. The press took that as an early sign that Yoko, either for personal or professional reasons, was being the aggressor in an imagined relationship with the Beatle. But as Yoko would jokingly remark to *Uncut*, the story was a whole lot of nothing. "There was this myth that I sent *Grapefruit* to him and how I wanted to trap him. The reality was that I had a large, orange carton of them that I would give out to critics. It was that sort of thing. He wasn't the only one who got a copy."

Despite Yoko's protests that there was nothing devious about sending Lennon a copy of *Grapefruit,* the book would have exactly that effect. The simplicity and directness of the lines in the book struck at something deeply philosophical and personal. It was the first sign of enchantment in the words and the woman who created them. Some weeks after receiving *Grapefruit*, Yoko received a phone call from Lennon, inviting her to his house for a chat about things. Yoko had no clue about Lennon's intent but went and although that initial get together would be fairly innocuous, focusing on Lennon's naivety about purchasing a lighthouse that appeared in materials enclosed with the book. They both had a giggle when Yoko broke the news to Lennon that the lighthouse was part of her conceptual art and did not exist in reality. But Yoko would leave that initial meeting sensing that there was a bit of a spark between them and sensed both fear and excitement at what could happen next.

What passed for a courtship would play out over the next year at a distance. Yoko was off at various points of the world with her growing reputation in the avant garde world while Lennon was finishing up the last wave of Beatles recordings. But whatever was going on in their lives, Yoko recalled in *Uncut* that Lennon always seemed to find time to call her.

"There were times when he would call me. I was always wondering why he would call me. He wasn't chatty. It was like "Hi." And then there would be silence. I wasn't that chatty either. There was a lot of silences in those phone calls."

In 1967, Yoko was casting about for funding for her latest project entitled Half a Wind, an exhibit in which furniture and other objects were cut in half and displayed. Yoko didn't think twice about asking Lennon for financial support even though she knew it would give further evidence to the world at large that she was pursuing Lennon strictly for money and to benefit from being in the same conversation with him. During conversations, Yoko found Lennon to be artistically astute and intellectually opinionated. She gushed to *Uncut* that, "It's not like he simply understood what I was trying to do. He was actually on the same wavelength."

All of which added to the growing attraction between them that Yoko would readily admit to years later in conversation with *Uncut*. "I had this feeling about John. Our feelings were getting close to danger. I knew we were kind of hot for each other by then."

They would continue to maintain a cautious distance over the next months, exchanging letters and phone conversations. And Yoko would acknowledge that what was going on was no secret to Lennon's wife Cynthia who was, in the declining stages of their marriage, well aware that her husband and Yoko had been in fairly constant communication.

The tensions between Lennon and Yoko would finally reach its apex in 1968 when Cynthia and some close friends went out of the country, leaving Lennon to his own devices. What happened next would be slashed across countless newspapers, magazines and books in often negative tones, painting Yoko as a home wrecker and much worse. Years later, Yoko would offer *Uncut* her version of the story.

"I was in London because of this concert I did with Ornette Coleman. John called and said 'Okay, shall we meet?' By then we both knew how we were feeling. I went there and he was waiting with change to pay the taxi. Once inside, John said 'We can do two things. One is just sit here and chat or we can go up [to his studio] and make music.' He didn't mean 'make music' in a funny way. He really meant make music. I said let's make music. So we went up to his attic and we made music that was to become *Two Virgins*. After that we made it [love]."

The next morning Yoko and Lennon were sitting together in bliss when Cynthia unexpectedly returned from her holiday and found them together. Over the years, that encounter has been exaggerated by the press to almost mythic proportions. Yoko offered as much when reflecting on that moment with *Uncut*.

"When Cynthia came in on us, I immediately tried to sit a little bit further away from John. John said 'No. Don't worry about it. It's okay.' He grabbed my hand and we were sitting together. He wanted it that way. I don't know why. He wasn't like 'My wife is coming and we have to hide the situation. Cynthia and the people she was with stayed a while, said hi and then left by the front door, not in a huff. There was an underlying tension but we were all civil.'"

The Yoko/Lennon relationship would move at lightning speed.

Divorce papers were filed by Cynthia accusing her husband of having an affair with Yoko. For her part, Yoko, likewise, divorced Cox. At that point, Yoko, truly free, had designs on living alone and concentrating on her art. But Lennon was intent that Yoko move in with him. Shortly after Lennon's divorce from Cynthia, Yoko discovered that she was pregnant.

Yoko had always been of two minds when it came to children and motherhood. Lennon was thrilled at the news and, as Yoko would discover in the ensuing years, was quick to make it public. Years later, Yoko would address her ongoing conflict between motherhood and career in *Chrissylley.com*. "I was a proud person, thinking my work was good. When I got pregnant, I had to concentrate on being pregnant even though I was ruining my career at the time."

During the earliest days of their relationship, Yoko was beginning to show Lennon that there were other emotional and spiritual choices available beyond the seeming limitations of pop music stardom. Lennon was smitten and, as such, was susceptible to Yoko's anti-war sentiments and how they might use their collective notoriety and it was noted that the couple would be seen in the crowds of several anti-Vietnam War rallies in 1968.

From the outset, Yoko would find herself at odds with Lennon's conservative upbringing that emphasized marriage and children. "I was never really ready to be a mother," she confessed to *Humanity Magazine*. "I just felt so much better when I was working on something creative."

Yoko's life during the early stages of the pregnancy was a blur of conflicting emotions. At this point, she was being constantly hounded and under attack by the press as the other woman who broke up Lennon's marriage and the earliest stories that she was not only manipulating Lennon in his final days with The Beatles but that she had also been instrumental in causing the breakup of the band.

To make matters worse, in October 1968, she would also suffer the stress and humiliation when Lennon and she were arrested and charged with drug possession. Confused and emotionally at odds, Yoko would, years later, admit to no small amount of anger that was creeping into her life. "I'm angry every day but I don't hold onto it because it will make me physically sick," she said in *Chrissylley.com*. "You don't keep it inside. You don't blame anybody."

But dealing with the anger and the inherent stress of the drug arrest was a contributing factors in Yoko having a miscarriage on November

21, 1968. Art and life would come together for Yoko and Lennon who, shortly before the miscarriage, would record the unborn baby's fetal heartbeat and, the following year would include the recording in the album *Life with the Lions* followed by two minutes of silence.

One month after the projected due date of the child who had been named John Ono Lennon II, the couple, now legally free from their respective spouses, were quietly married on March 20, 1969 on the Isle of Gibraltar in Spain.

Prior to the actual ceremony, Yoko and Lennon would spend what they termed a pre-honeymoon in Paris, seeing the sights and, along the way, falling deeply in love. In the book *Lennon* by Ray Coleman, Yoko acknowledged the experience when she said, "When people get cynical about love, they should look at us and see that it is possible."

Needless to say, the marriage was world news and well attended by hordes of international press. It was during the ceremony that Yoko, anti-establishment and progressive thinker to a fault, found herself succumbing to the traditions of marriage. "I got so emotional at the wedding that I broke down and John nearly did too," she said in the book *Lennon*. "The man who married us was rabbiting on about 'Do you take this woman for your wife.' It was a tremendous experience."

The wedding was also a time for Yoko to begin to exert her independence and opinion and she found the notoriously defiant and conservative Lennon willing to go to any lengths to succumb to her wishes. In the book *Lennon*, she related how, around the time of the marriage, she approached Lennon and told him "I don't like being known as Mrs. Lennon. How would you like it if you had to change your name upon marriage to Mr. John Ono. So some weeks after the marriage, John legally changed his middle name from Winston to Ono."

In what would be their first act of in-your face social and political defiance, the couple created a honeymoon event dubbed Bed-Ins for Peace, a two week sleep-in to protest the Vietnam War and all conflicts in general that took place in The Hilton in Amsterdam and The Queen Elizabeth Hotel in Montreal. "We thought Amsterdam was a very important place to do it," she told *Ultimate Classic Rock*," because Amsterdam had a very fresh and alive interest. And we were thinking that, instead of going out and fighting and making war or something like that, we should just stay in bed."

The bed-ins were an international sensation, drawing the press, fans and fellow political and social travelers, as Yoko and Lennon, dressed in pajamas, would entertain the press amid signs and slogans of protest. Part protest and part social experiment, the bed-ins were often the butt of what the press perceived as a put on and a joke. Yoko would look back on the bed-ins in both social and artistic terms in an interview with *MOMA Retrospective* and the book *Come Together: John Lennon and His Time* by Jan Weiner.

"John and I thought after The Bed Ins, the war was going to end. But things take time. It's just taking a little bit more time than we thought it would back then. People were making fun of what we were doing but it was part of our policy not to be taken seriously. Our opposition didn't know how to handle humor."

Following the bed-ins, Yoko and Lennon would set about their lives together in a largely creative and productive manner.

Between 1968-69 their first musical efforts as a couple, with Yoko's influence and Lennon's emotional turn to a more introspective/ progressive lifestyle and an immediate obsession with his love for Yoko took flight. The first two albums in this collaboration, *Unfinished Music No. 1 Two Virgins* and *Unfinished Music No. 2 Life with the Lions*, were totally experimental and avant-garde, consisting of tape loops, disjointed snippets of music and vocals and random musings about things in their lives. Both barely charted and the lion's share of the notoriety was of the naked picture of Lennon and Yoko on the cover. *Wedding Album* would, by degrees, be more coherent than the previous two efforts but also, like *Two Virgins* and *Life with the Lions*, would be both a critical and commercial failure

But what these albums did attest to was that Yoko was having a growing influence on Lennon's creative and feminist side. Yoko would be direct in her prodding of her husband to go more minimalist and autobiographical, providing musical and creative links to her Fluxus art period from years gone by. But Yoko would be more diplomatic and circumspect when she addressed her influence on Lennon as a student/teacher relationship.

"I think the fact that we were together had something to do with it." Yoko explained to *Esquire*. "I wasn't doing what he [John] was doing and he wasn't doing what I was doing. We didn't have any plans. He just did it and I just did it. We didn't fight about it. It worked very well that way."

However, Yoko would hint at her feminine ways as an element in any creative sway she may have had over Lennon in *The Complete*

Playboy Interviews book. "Maybe it's that I have a strength, a feminine strength. I think that women really have the inner wisdom."

What seemed like an idyllic, albeit unconventional, marriage continued to be marred by Yoko's inability to conceive and give birth to Lennon's child. Yoko addressed the problem in a conversation with *Humanity*. "John was so adamant about having a child with me. He would say 'We have to have a child. We have to.' I ended up having some miscarriages and everyone around us was saying 'well she just can't hold it.'"

The late 60's through the early 70's were a time of growth and experimentation in and out of the relationship for Yoko. She was at Lennon's side as he took his first formative steps away from the Beatles with recordings and live performances. Yoko took this period to venture into the uncharted waters of recording with a pair of albums *Yoko Ono: Plastic Ono Band* (1970) and *Fly* (1971). It came as no surprise that both albums were very avant-garde, harkening back to her Fluxus art period and, by association totally out of sync with commercial realities, despite the contributions and encouragement of Lennon that were slowly bringing a sense of rock n'roll structure to the proceedings.

Yoko would assess her creative turmoil during the recording of those albums in conversation with *Rolling Stone*. "I was doing music in my mind, no sound at all and everybody sitting around just imagining sounds. I felt stifled. I was dying to scream, to go back to my voice. I came to a point where I believed that the idea of avante garde purity was just as stifling as a rock beat over and over."

But while critics of her early work were dismissive and often downright nasty of her early albums, Yoko remained steadfast in her belief that her art was paramount. "Art to me is a way of showing people how you think," she explained to *The Guardian*. "Some people think that art is beautiful wallpaper that you can sell. But I have always thought that it had to do with activism. To be an artist you need courage and most people don't think like that."

With that kind of attitude, it was little wonder that when the celebrity couple took to hanging out in radically and politically charged circles with the likes of Bobbie Seale, Abbie Hoffman, Jerry Rubin and Angela Davis, it was often Yoko who took the lead in discourse when the topic turned to sexism, racism and in her support of feminism. Yoko had always been very much her own person and was never shy about making her opinions known. "He [John] always had the intention to better the world and I was like that too," she quipped to *The Guardian*.

And there would be a price to be paid for her activism and attitude. Charges that she was responsible for breaking up The Beatles had begun too as well as the hostility during their more activist days and because of what many perceived as the unorthodox creative direction Lennon was indulging in.

Yoko would deflect the anti-Yoko sentiment in an interview with *CNN* when she said, "The hostility directed toward me was sort of like a distant thing in a way because John and I were so close. We were just totally involved in each other and our work." But there was also a sense of growing frustration at being everybody's favorite target as she explained to *Biography*. "Can you imagine everyday getting this vibration of hate from people? I wanted to get out of that."

She also wanted to get out of what had turned into a rapidly deteriorating life with Lennon. The album she and Lennon had worked together on, *Sometimes In New York City*, had been a commercial failure with many openly predicting the end of Lennon's career. On one occasion she sat in a room listening as her drunken husband had sex with another woman. At the time, Yoko was locked in a prolonged legal battle with her ex-husband for custody of their daughter. Adding to the malaise that had become Yoko's day-to-day life was the fact that her husband had descended to become a self-centered and quite needy man.

"John didn't even want me to go to the bathroom by myself," an exasperated Yoko recalled in an interview with *The Telegraph*. "'I will come with you' he would say and this would be in public places. All I could think of was that sometimes a girl has to piss alone."

Yoko's mind took a progressive turn. In her mind, Lennon needed some time alone to feel what it was like to be alone in an uncertain world. "I noticed that he was beginning to become a bit more restless," she told *Biography*. "I thought it was better to give him a rest and to give me a rest."

But not before she made the daring move of making sure he would not be alone in their separation. And so it was that Yoko literally arranged for her assistant May Pang to follow Lennon and to become his lover. "May Pang was a very intelligent, attractive woman and extremely efficient," she told *Biography*. "I thought they'd be okay together."

Years later, Pang, in conversation with *The Independent*, painted

Yoko as both calculating and controlling when she described how Yoko had approached her to go with Lennon. "She said 'I know you don't have a boyfriend and you would be good with him [Lennon]. I said 'I didn't think so' but she said 'You don't want him to go out with somebody who is going to be nasty to him, do you?' I said 'Of course not' and she said 'You will be perfect' and walked out."

Between 1973 and 75, Yoko and Lennon would live apart and live very different lives. Lennon would quickly become a drunken clown, making his home in Los Angeles and creating unhealthy headlines on an almost daily basis with fights, extreme intoxication and overall behavior unbecoming a famous celebrity while managing two well-received albums, *Walls And Bridges* and *Rock N' Roll*. For Yoko, it was a time for contemplation and creativity. Being alone was a welcome break from the past years of chaotic love and often brutal public scrutiny. And as she would acknowledge in a *Pitchfork.com* article, she had learned a lot.

"What I learned from being with John is that society suddenly treated me as a woman that belonged to a man. Some of John's closest friends told me that I should just stay in the background, that I should just shut up, I should just give up my work and that way I would be happy. I was lucky. I was over 30 and it was too late for me to change."

The result of their time apart would result in what many consider one of Yoko's underappreciated albums, *Feeling the Space*. The album, quite simply, was Yoko's take on feminism, done up in direct creeds like "Woman Power," "She Hits Back," "Yellow Girl (Stand By For Life)" and "Angry Young Woman." Easily her most personal musical statement to that point, and sadly one that followed Yoko's previous albums into obscurity, *Feeling the Space* had the distinction of, musically, being one of her most polished efforts, combining her lyrics with a close to commercial sound courtesy of a host of name session musicians and one interloper who went by the name of John O'Cean who played guitar on the songs "Woman Power," "She Hits Back" and sang a single background vocal line on the song "Men, Men, Men." John O'Cean was, in fact, John Lennon, who, after his much publicized tantrums and run-ins with the law because of his political activism, was attempting a musical comeback of his own with the album *Mind Games*.

Lennon's contributions were a sign that Yoko and he had, despite the separation, remained on good terms. The reality was, according to Yoko in a *Biography.com* interview, was that they had remained in contact almost from the day they split. "We missed each other. We were calling each other every day. Some days he would call me three or four times. I was prepared to lose him but I didn't think I would lose him. It was better that he came back."

But while Lennon himself conceded in a *Playboy* interview that he had literally begged Yoko to take him back, Yoko, who in the previous months had come to like the idea of being on her own, was philosophical and cautious when she looked back on them reuniting during a *Playboy* interview. "It had slowly dawned on me that John was not the trouble at all [in our relationship]. It was society that had become too much [for us]. We started dating again but I wanted to be sure."

But as Yoko and Lennon would discover, there was not enough time to proceed with caution. Shortly after they reunited and began dating, the couple had a surprise that would test Yoko. "We'd just gotten back together and I became pregnant very soon," she said in a *BBC Radio 4* interview. "I know it sounds strange now but I thought 'well I should let John decide whether to keep it or not.' I didn't know if it was the right moment to have a child because maybe he didn't want it. I didn't want to burden him with something he didn't want. He said 'of course we're going to keep it' and he was really upset with my remark."

Given Yoko's history of miscarriages, the couple would remain extremely cautious during the coming months. Lennon would be the dutiful husband and father to be, often pushing Yoko around their New York apartment (The Dakota) in a wheelchair. Yoko would give birth to Sean Taro Ono Lennon on October 9, 1975. The irony of the son coming into the world on the same day his father was born was not lost on the couple.

There was a sense of new life and a new beginning in the air. And one that would change both Yoko and Lennon's lives forever. After years of being on the hamster wheel of fame and, literally and figuratively, under contract to deliver for most of his adult life, Lennon made the decision to take a hiatus from music and anything that had to do with a professional life and become a house husband, dedicating every waking hour to seeing to the care and feeling of his son and being the caretaker of the house.

Yoko was fine with her husband's decision. There was something about Lennon's willingness to give up his career to cook and clean that appealed to her feminist side. But where did that leave Yoko? Where it left her was that she was suddenly designated to make sense of Lennon and her financial holdings, which, on the surface, seemed massive. There was income generated from many areas connected to The Beatles and Apple (the Beatles' Corporate arm) and more recent real estate investments. Yoko was more than willing to venture into the alien world of money and economics. And the first thing she discovered was that while they were well off, they were not super rich.

"Being connected to Apple and all the lawyers and bankers who have a piece of us, we didn't know how much money we had and we weren't financially independent," she told *Newsweek*. But perhaps the most significant challenge facing Yoko was that, initially, no one was taking her seriously as the money person in this newly constituted lifestyle. Lawyers and bankers would regularly send important papers directly to Lennon or his legal representatives.

Yoko saw this as blatant sexism by old, white establishment types. And as she would discover during this period, so did the public as she offered in an interview with *Playboy*. "When John and I would go out, people would come up and say 'John, what are you doing?' But they never asked about me because, as a woman, I wasn't supposed to be doing anything."

Yoko persisted and eventually the old school money people, most likely grudgingly, came around to the reality that Yoko was now the money person in the Lennon family. "I handled the business, the old business and the new investments, " she said in a *Playboy* interview. " I learned. The law is not a mystery to me anymore. Politicians are not a mystery to me anymore. I'm not scared of all that establishment stuff anymore."

There would be a flurry of activity as the couple prepared for their role reversal. Lennon released the album *Shaved Fish*, his last album on his final contract and was now officially without a label. He worked with Ringo for a short time in the studio but, after that, he was officially free and would spend the next five years at home, changing Sean's diapers and baking bread. Yoko would often marvel at the decision, as she offered in *Harper's Bazaar*.

"John felt I knew more about business, which was not true. So he wanted me to take care of the business and he wanted to take care of the child, which was an incredible thing. In those days, nobody did that. It was a macho age. And John cooked. He baked bread."

This domestic arrangement seemed to defy the odds for the first few years. Yoko had grown quite confident in dealing with the business aspects of their lives and Lennon seemed quite content in the role of house-husband. While Lennon had reportedly taken a hiatus from everything creative, he would occasionally dabble in some very basic songwriting, fragments of which never saw the light of day. Yoko was fine with Lennon's attempts but after a time noticed that he had become quite listless and lethargic in the face of his newfound role. She would encourage him to take the occasional trip to unwind and it would be on a boat excursion to Bermuda in 1980 that Lennon once again was inspired to write real songs. It turned out that Yoko had also been writing and so, when Lennon returned to New York inspired and ready to record, Yoko's contributions resulted in what would become *Double Fantasy*, a musical love letter that included a number of Yoko songs.

Excited at the idea of Lennon recording and including some of her material, Yoko, nevertheless, was generous in defending *Double Fantasy* as Lennon driven in a *The Spokesman Review.com* interview. "I have two concerns for this album. First I hope that it reminds people of John's talent. Second, I hope that the fact that I'm working with him enhances the man-woman dialogue."

Upon its release, *Double Fantasy* seemed to strike a chord with even the most hard bitten of observers. The tone of a deep felt relationship between Lennon and Yoko was sincere, successfully walking the tightrope between schmaltzy and real. It was a daring album on a number of fronts, dancing occasionally around the concept of being commercial with very real emotion stripped to the bone. Lennon and Yoko had taken a big risk in putting all their emotional cards on the table and the result was more success than the couple had seen since they began working together.

But upon release on November 17, 1980, *Double Fantasy* appeared to be yet another uphill climb for Yoko and Lennon. The album would reach gold status fairly quickly but critics could not seem to get past the couple's idealism and the ego involved in putting out an entire album centered around their relationship. Reviews would remain mixed, with many continuing to blame Yoko for the unpopular direction that Lennon's music was going, according to critics. That the album remained frustratingly stalled did not seem to dampen the spirits of Yoko and Lennon who, in interviews, were quite upbeat in what *Double Fantasy* had accomplished.

December 8, 1980 would be a busy day. Lennon and Yoko would

spend the day doing interviews and posing for photographer Annie Liebowitz for a *Rolling Stone* magazine cover. At 4:50 pm, the couple would go to the nearby recording studio where they would spend approximately five hours fine-tuning the song "Walking On Thin Ice." The couple were upbeat as they left the studio and made their way back to The Dakota. Yoko, in an *Access.com* interview, remembered the night well.

"We were returning from the studio and I said 'Should we go and have dinner before we go home?' And John kept saying 'No, let's go home because I want to see Sean before he goes to sleep.' It was like he wasn't sure if we could get home before he went to sleep and he was concerned about that."

As they reached The Dakota, Lennon and Yoko were confronted by a fan named Mark David Chapman. It was the second time they had encountered Chapman that day. Earlier he had approached them and asked Lennon to sign his copy of *Double Fantasy*. Lennon recognized him but being the very outgoing, friendly person he had morphed into in recent years, he did not see Chapman as anything more than a persistent fan. Chapman pulled a gun, dropped into a combat shooting position and fired five shots into Lennon, hitting him four times in the back and once in the chest. Lennon staggered a few feet toward The Dakota entrance and then crumbled to the ground.

Lennon was rushed to a nearby hospital and was declared dead at 11:15 p.m.

Yoko was in a state of shock as was just about the entire world. Spontaneous gatherings took place and grief lined the faces of literally millions. By 11:16, Yoko had taken the first emotional steps of being the widow of one of the most revered people on the planet. "When John died I thought it was the worst thing that would ever happen," she told interviewer Vicki Sheff. "But that was only the beginning."

Within hours, Yoko gave formal instructions to have John Lennon's body immediately cremated. Shortly afterward, she broke the news to her son Sean. Being quite young, Sean did not completely understand the concept of his father being taken from him. He wanted to know why his father had been shot. Yoko did not have an answer.

Yoko had long ago become comfortable with being able to walk the streets without any semblance of security but, in the hours following Lennon's murder, she suddenly found herself dealing with her grief while suddenly surrounded by security, law enforcement, and the presence of a handful of confidants who were acting as a buffer between her and an outside world that was suddenly going crazy with grief and insanity. Within 24 hours, there would be bomb threats and at least one call that indicated that another killer was on his way to finish Chapman's work. Inevitably, there would be extremist speculation, the most egregious being that Yoko had Lennon killed. During those first emotionally fragile days, Yoko would, by degrees, communicate with those who were grieving at Lennon's loss. When several Lennon followers reportedly killed themselves following the news, Yoko made a statement telling millions to not take their own lives.

In the few private moments that played out over the ensuing weeks, Yoko would often be found sitting alone in quiet contemplation. At other times she would just break down and cry. The media, now frantic in any angle on the tragedy, would dig out old quotes from Yoko regarding her personal karma as a jumping off point to speculate that her karma may well have been a contributing factor to Lennon's demise. Years later, Yoko would deflect what she considered an absurdist theory when she was quoted in *The Express.com* as saying "No, my karma did not affect John. John's death was just the worst of everything."

There would be more challenges for Yoko in the coming years.

With Lennon's death, Yoko was now the de facto manager of Lennon's estate and holdings worth an estimated $150 million. It would be a financial legacy that would have people coming out of the woodwork with their hands out. Yoko was bombarded with demands from people who claimed to have been owed money by Lennon and, in some cases, they hinted that they would hold Lennon memorabilia in lieu of payment. There would continue to be countless and dubious lawsuits and flat out begging from strangers washing up on Yoko's doorstep. It would not be long before she was bombarded by authors seeking her participation in books that, not surprisingly, were in various stages of rushed development. And, in the darkest of dark ironies, she even received a letter from Lennon's killer, Mark David Chapman, wanting to know where she would like the proceeds from a book he was considering doing to go.

All of which seemingly left little time to privately consider her mental and emotional well being in dealing with Lennon's death. In conversation with *BBC.com* she went so far as to consider that Lennon

127

was, in her heart and soul, very much alive. "He's still alive. He's still with us. His spirit will go on. You can't kill a person that easily."

But while speaking of Lennon in lofty and spiritual terms shortly after his death, Yoko would quickly evolve into a psychological realist when it came to dealing with the tragedy. In an excerpt from *The Express.com* article, she was quoted as telling those handling the media in those early days to "Just be truthful about the situation and to not try to turn John into some kind of saint or martyr." She would be much harsher some years later when she told the *Tampa Bay Times* that, "As a mother, I told myself I gotta' survive. John died. He was killed. If he wasn't John Lennon, he would not have been killed. Work is consoling and gives you strength but without your family, who needs you? Some days I felt like life wasn't worth it. But it was important that I stay around for Sean or he would have ended up losing two parents."

Within a year, Yoko was showing signs of coming out of her grief period. She became romantically involved with a man named Sam Havadtoy, 19 years younger than Yoko and, perhaps more important, she released her first album since Lennon's death entitled *Season of Glass*, a stark emergence into the emotions and demons that had been stalking her. The album cover, which featured a photo of Lennon's blood spattered glasses and a primal acknowledgement of that horrible moment in the song '*No, No, No*'. Many accused her of exploiting her husband's death but Yoko shook the attacks off. After all, she had long ago gotten used to being 'The Dragon Lady'.

The decade of the 80's continued to follow Yoko on a myriad of musical and artistic journeys. The albums *It's Alright (I See Rainbows)* and *Starpeace* highlighted a myriad of interests in exploring social, political and, yes, biographical insights into just what makes an artist tick. The odyssey continued into the 90's with the albums *Rising* and *A Story*.

There would be a belated recognition of Yoko as a pioneering conceptual artist, musician and performer, influencing and recording with many younger performers and finding her way in the world at a time when those entering their later years, especially those with a strong celebrity/pop culture past, are pulling back from the public eye. If anything, as she has aged, Yoko has become even more optimistic.

"I do feel that I'm starting over a new life," she told *The Guardian*, "a second life that will have so many things." She is thrilled that, going into her 80's that she still has a full life with nonstop meetings and participation in so many things. "Thank God, I have all this work to do," she offered to *TheGentlewoman.com*. "It's such a blessing because when you're working, you find all this new energy. It's very important to not just live by the clock. I don't do that anymore. I just work, work, work."

But it would be more than just the act of doing that was driving Yoko. After all these years, Yoko had become an international toast of the town, fueled in all candor by her celebrity status/Lennon connection and she would be the recipient of countless gallery retrospectives and exhibitions. Through it all, Yoko remained the purist when it came to discussing her passion in *InspiringQuotes.com*. "Art is like breathing for me. If I don't do it, I start to choke."

Over the years, Yoko would take part in endless ceremonies and exhibitions tied to her late husband. Some days living in the memory of John Lennon and his impact on the world, could be stressful. The legacy, creatively and personally, could be overwhelming. But there was much in Yoko's life with Lennon that brought the glow of remembrance and so made her role as caretaker for a departed legend a welcome chore.

"I loved his tenderness," she offered the *Tampa Bay Times*. "I loved his affectionate nature. He was also a person who tried to be honest with himself and he really worked at it. When fans see his life, maybe they see that anything is possible."

One thing that has eluded Yoko in her later years has been romance. Although Yoko and Sam Havadtoy had long ago admitted to being in a relationship, to what degree that lingers has long been the subject of conjecture. But Yoko would go so far as to concede that well into her 70's, there were no romantic relationships in her life. "It's difficult," she admitted to *TheGentlewoman.com*. "I just think that it's great that I'm alone now because to involve any guy in this strange life I live, they'd have to give up so much. Or if they didn't give it up, it would be very difficult for me."

And so when not out in the public eye these days, Yoko lives and enjoys living in her head and living a solitary existence. "I love walking early in the morning when people are on their way to the office and not bothering me," she told *TheGentlewoman.com*. "Or at dusk with a bodyguard. Even then it's not easy to walk around because I get hassled so I tend to stay home and read a lot."

In 2020, Yoko, on the occasion of her 87th birthday, began to show signs of physically breaking down. When she was seen in public, it was often in a wheelchair being pushed by her son Sean or laboring to walk with the use of a cane. During an award acceptance speech that same year, it was reported by several news outlets including *Fox News* and the *New York Post* that Yoko hinted at learning to live with "an illness" which she was not specific about and, subsequently, nobody would talk about. But it was also reported at that time that Yoko now required 24 hour in home care and that she had begun to sell off some of her real estate holdings.

However, those in her inner circle would insist that Yoko was still sharp as a tack and was maintaining, to the degree she could, as a public personality, contributing to various charities and making appearances at ceremonies honoring her or John Lennon. Yoko seemed at peace and, typically Yoko, she seemed at ease with her long, often controversial but, ultimately rewarding life and was looking forward to the future with *TheGentlewoman.com.*

"I don't know how long I'm going to live but my prediction is that we will have heaven on earth in the year 2050. When I tell people this, they 'Oh, but you won't be here in 2050.'

And I say 'Well who knows?'"

Chapter Seven
Olivia Arias/Harrison

December 30, 1999. 3:00 a.m.

Moments before, George Harrison had gone downstairs to investigate what sounded like a break-in in progress and had come face to face with Michael Abram, a former heroin addict and mental patient who was convinced that The Beatles were witches and that they had to die. At one point in the confrontation, Abram lunged at George with a knife and punctured a lung. As they struggled and George cried out for help, his blood spattered the walls.

Olivia heard the sounds of the struggle and George's cries for help. Racing into the hallway, Olivia found a weapon in the form of a brass poker and ran downstairs and came face to face with George's bloodied body and the crazy person trying to take his life.

"I've never seen my husband look like that," she reported in a trial testimony excerpted in the book *Behind Sad Eyes: The Life of George Harrison.* "I raised my hand and hit the man on the head as many times as I could, as hard as I could."

At one point in the struggle, Abram knocked Olivia to the ground but she quickly recovered and continued to beat Abram in the head until he slumped to the ground. In a court transcript, Olivia's spirituality came through as she described the aftermath of the attack. "George and I were saved by desperation, love of one another and the grace of God."

Exhibit A. Olivia Harrison was a fighter in more ways than one and she had come by that reputation long before that fateful night in 1999. In the aftermath of that violent encounter, Olivia's close friend Elizabeth Emanuel declared in *Behind Sad Eyes: The Life of George Harrison,* that Olvia's reaction was not a surprise. "She's fit and strong. I would imagine she would be very brave in those circumstances. She's quite tough."

Unlike many of the Beatle wives, Olivia immediately impressed those in George Harrison's inner circle as a tough, no nonsense, no bullshit woman who was far from a shrinking violet, who had opinions and was not above making them known, and in all matters of emotion and deed stood out as a very different mate to a quite famous man. As was offered in *Behind Sad Eyes: The Life of George Harrison*. "Olivia was a woman of the earth. She had simple tastes and simple ideals." Olivia was not overly impressed by the trappings of celebrity and was a realist in dealing with life's challenges. All of which would make her distinctive in the pantheon of Beatle wives.

The late musician Tom Petty got to know Olivia during The Traveling Wilburys days and, as he offered in a heartfelt *Rolling Stone* interview, was impressed. "When I heard about it [the break-in] I sent George a fax and it just said 'Aren't you glad you married a Mexican girl?' She really kicked ass. She is a beautiful person. Olivia had the hardest job in the world because she loved George. She took care of him, cleared the path in front of him and behind him and inherited that crazy life."

While others have seemingly stood in line to praise Olivia's tenacity and real world nature, Olivia seemed to have little to say when assessing her own character through much of her years with Harrison, preferring to stay behind the scenes. But with the death of Harrison, Olivia was seemingly pushed to the forefront as spokeswoman for Harrison's vast holdings and legacy. It was in that stage of her life, and in conjunction with promoting a major film documentary of Harrison's life and times, that Olivia dropped some hints as to what she was made of in an interview with *Rolling Stone*.

"I have an overdeveloped sense of duty," she offered. "Being in the spotlight, it's not what I want to do. It's not a carrot for me but by default I have to be the one. I'm not talking to everyone and I'm saying no to a lot. I do not want to be on television and I am not a celebrity."

Olivia Trinidad Arias was born on May 18, 1948 in Los Angeles, the second of five children born to Zeke and Mary Louise Arias, whose roots were deeply ingrained in Mexico largely due to their parents' life in the Mexican region of Guanajuato. Olivia would hear the stories of how the onset of the Mexican Revolution led her parents to come to the United States for a better life.

But she also recalled in a *MoreLAFilmfest.com* interview that she grew up with a keen sense of her Mexican roots. "My father was a singer and guitarist who played guitar and sang professionally for a time in the 1930's. I grew up watching Mexican films and listening to Mexican music. I haven't spent much time in Mexico but it is really where my heart is."

The family settled in Hawthorne, California, a suburb of Los Angeles with a large Mexican population. Olivia's early years are hard to decipher. On the surface, she seemed a happy child, prone to shyness and a bit on the quiet side. But the fact was that her father, a dry cleaner and her mother, a seamstress, were not always around, owing to the reality of having to make a living for their ever-expanding family. This would put Olivia, at a fairly early age, at odds with her life and lifestyle as she would acknowledge in a *Daily Telegraph* interview. "We lived only about 10 miles from Beverly Hills but it was a different world. There was a very affluent society that I didn't even know existed. For a long time, I thought we were poor. I had love, support and as much, materially, as my parents could give. It's just that my parents were never there because they were always working and, as a child, you want your mother and father around."

Olivia learned to live and function quite well within the family dynamic and, by all accounts, grew up, thanks to a warm and loving family environment, a normal and seemingly unaffected child. Olivia entered Hawthorne High School in the fall of 1961. The school was largely known as the place where the Beach Boys attended as well as a slightly lesser celebrity, Chris Montez, who had a string of top ten hits in the early 60's. Montez was friends with Olivia's older brother and would often cross paths with Olivia when he would come by the Arias household.

Montez, in conversation with the website *PleaseKillMe.com*, recalled "I was friends with Ron Arias [Olivia's older brother] and we'd hang out a lot. I used to go to his house all the time. He had this little sister. She would always smile and was kind of shy. That was Olivia."

Olivia's high school anecdotes would be fragmentary at best. She had a group of friends she hung out with, was heavily into music and a big Beatles fan, having seen the band perform live in 1965. And although she would never come out and say it, she would occasionally drop hints of experiencing subtle racism during her high school years. "I always knew I was not going to be one of the cheerleaders with a little skirt and I had a feeling it was because I was brown," she told the *Daily Telegraph*.

Olivia graduated from Hawthorne High School in 1965. She was not quite sure what was next. There was the possibility of college. But she was also aware that her superior shorthand and typing skills made her a natural in the job market. She would choose the latter and spent the next eight years working at various secretarial positions. Between 1971 and 1972, Olivia took a self-imposed vacation in Europe. She would look at this time as a rite of passage, excited and confident on her own on the other side of the world.

Technology was still in its infancy and so it was while in Europe, Olivia heard about *The Concert for Bangladesh,* after the fact. "I remembered being annoyed that I didn't know about the concert and thinking how could I have missed that?" she recalled to *The Independent.*

Upon returning to the states, Olivia landed a secretarial job in the merchandising department of A&M Records. Over that first year at A&M, Olivia impressed the company with her industrious, conscientious and no nonsense approach to the work at hand. She was so on top of things that in 1973 when A&M was in serious negotiations to pick up distribution rights to George Harrison's newly formed *Dark Horse Records*, Olivia's attention to detail and being on top of every aspect of the business made her the logical choice to be go between Harrison and A&M.

It would be a matter of luck, timing and karma because, at that time, Olivia had just handed in her notice at A&M and was ready to move to an Ashram in Colorado to further her life and spiritual journey when she received a phone call from Harrison's then manager, asking her to come to work for Harrison and Dark Horse Records. A firm believer in situations presenting themselves for a reason, Olivia immediately said yes to the offer.

Not surprisingly, Harrison was at wits end at the time Olivia came into the picture. He was up to his neck in finishing the album *Dark Horse* and auditioning musicians for an upcoming tour. Adding to that was the extensive business side of forming his own label Dark Horse that Harrison had to learn on the fly. Harrison was the first to admit that he was in over his head and that he needed help.

In conversations with Olivia during the prolonged negotiations with A&M to distribute Dark Horse Records, he immediately found Olivia to be a stabilizing element in his chaotic world. Olivia was all business, had answers to all his questions and made immediate points in Harrison's mind at being seemingly in control at all times.

Olivia assessed her immediate connection with Harrison in those early days in conversation with the *Buffalo News*. "I was from outside his world. I was simple and he needed some kind of simple in his life at that point."

But she would point out years later in conversation with *The Sun* that it quickly evolved into something else beyond a simple work connection. "It was pretty much love at first sight. We felt it in our hearts even before we met. We seemed to have some understanding like you do when you meet the right person."

While he was loath to admit it, Harrison was becoming infatuated as well. The calls, often instigated by Harrison, were becoming less about business and more personal. In Olivia, he was discovering a strong woman who was in sync with the real world that was more than balanced out by a spiritual and soulful side. He was well on the way to developing an emotional attachment. But he knew he had to be careful.

Harrison had been through a lot of women who, at the end of the day, used their connection to him for material gain or as a career boost. And so, on the heels of a chaotic breakup with Pattie and an equally dysfunctional love life, he was not going to take any chances. Using connections in California, he not too delicately asked that they check Olivia out. The search resulted in Olivia not having any deep, dark secrets or hidden agendas. They would continue their long distance phone relationship, discovering along the way, at least to Harrison's way of thinking, that Olivia was emotionally and spiritually his match, a woman who could be nurturing as well as real world savvy and the ideal counter to Harrison's often introspective and reclusive nature.

In a 2005 interview with *The Telegraph*, Olivia would vehemently dispute the charge that Harrison was having people check her out. "Oh that's funny! That is so far from the truth. George did say to his friend 'go check her out.' But he didn't mean to investigate me. He was flirting."

In hindsight, Olivia would be the ideal emotional tonic for Harrison according to musician and close Harrison friend Jim Keltner in a *Mojo* interview. "Olivia came into the picture at just the right time, a crazy dark time. She is a strong person and when he [Harrison] fell for her, we all agreed that it was a good thing. It wasn't good for him to be on his own and without her things would have gotten worse."

Olivia recalled to *Rolling Stone* how the pair unofficially met for the first time in October 1974 when Harrison flew to California, not long after the distribution deal with *Dark Horse* was finalized to inspect the *Dark Horse* offices and to iron out the logistics of his first *Dark Horse* solo album and upcoming tour.

"Nobody organized a welcoming party so I dashed out to the parking lot to greet him. I thought somebody should. He drove onto the lot by himself in this little car. I thought 'This is a big day in his life' and so I went outside and said welcome. He said 'what's going on?' He was very excited but it was just me."

Olivia recalled her first impressions of Harrison in humane terms with *The Sun*. "He was a terribly sweet person and I thought he needed a pal. He had a lot going on and there were a lot of demands. We quickly became good friends."

To the extent that, shortly after meeting him for the first time, Harrison presented Olivia with a gift that only a rock star could provide, a blue tinted picture of her eyes that would appear as part of the album cover of the *Dark Horse* album. "That was so sweet of him," she told *The Sun*. "One day he said 'Somebody is coming over to take a picture.' I'd only known him for a couple of weeks so it was like 'Oh, I think we're getting somewhere here.'"

While Olivia insists this was the first time they met face to face, a persistent alternative timeline claims that Harrison and Olivia met for the first time at a party, reportedly a year later and then became romantically involved. Olivia's version, upon further examination, seems to make more sense because by November 2, 1974, Olivia was George's constant companion/label representative, in particular, on the November 2-December 20 tour that featured Indian legend Ravi Shankar as his opening act.

For Olivia, the tour would be an indication of the emotional ups and downs to come. Harrison had been dealing with the disillusionment of his marriage to Pattie Boyd as well as the rigors of mounting the first solo tour by a former Beatle in North America. What she would see was Harrison physically and emotionally rundown and prone to being gregarious or withdrawn at a moment's notice. All of which was coming into play mere months into their relationship. But as the world would discover, Olivia was totally up to the task of propping up the truly sensitive, creative and erratic person she had fallen in love with.

She would tend to ignore his often boorish behavior and was quick to both admonish him for feeling sorry for himself and encouraging him to get on with his life. Even though it was very early in their relationship, the spiritually inclined Olivia was being true to the chestnut of marriage, 'in sickness and in health' and was constantly at Harrison's side to support, encourage and, as the occasion would often require, give him a verbal kick in the ass.

By that time, it was very much out there that they were in love and that Harrison was only waiting for his previous relationship to be legally resolved as he offered in *Record Disc And Mirror*. "We can't talk about marriage yet because I'm still married to Patti. But Olivia is my woman. Everyone knows I only want to be with her."

The couple retreated to Harrison's Friar Park home following the tour in 1974 and what would be three years of globetrotting meeting celebrities, working on subsequent albums and just being a pop culture icon. It was an eye opening lifestyle change for Olivia but one she kept at arm's length as she remained focused on the emotional care and feeding of her man. Which would be a constant in her life.

Based on the mediocre reviews of Harrison's first tour and the less than spectacular results of a follow up album, *Extra Texture*, Harrison had been driven into seclusion, spending more time tending his garden than doing any truly creative work. When he began to lose an unhealthy amount of weight and his skin began to show an unhealthy yellow hue, Harrison turned to religion and a seemingly endless amount of chanting to cure his ills.

By 1976, Olivia was growing frantic at Harrison's deteriorating health and insisted that her partner see a real doctor. Harrison stubbornly declined the suggestion, insisting that prayer would ultimately cure him. But Olivia was having none of it. Unbeknownst to Harrison, Olivia did some research on her own and discovered a California based acupuncturist who was renowned for his ability to cure sickness with the ancient art. Olivia insisted that Harrison see the doctor and, after Olivia not too delicately insisting that maybe prayer was not the answer, Harrison reluctantly agreed to travel to California and submit to acupuncture treatments. Within months, Harrison's physical and emotional outlook had taken a turn for the better.

Olivia's persistence had literally saved Harrison's life.

In December 1977, Harrison's return to the good life was complete when Olivia announced that she was pregnant with Harrison's first child. That Harrison was thrilled was obvious. That he was also quite relieved to have one particular monkey off his back was also palpable. During his marriage to Pattie, their inability to have children had been an embarrassment that Harrison once went public with by saying that their inability to have children was his fault not Pattie's, fueling the long held rumor that he was incapable of fathering children.

The couple was intent on doing things in a logical manner. One month after discovering the pregnancy, Olivia and Harrison were married on September 2, 1978 in a private ceremony at the Henley on Thames Register Office in England. Dhani Harrison was born December 1, 1978. Following the ceremony, the couple retreated to the Friar Park home for a period of quiet entrenchment in which the proud parents welcomed their son and a period of calm in which Olivia was the ideal wife and mother and Harrison, now creatively inspired, released a more upbeat, pop flavored album entitled *33 1/3* to favorable reviews and sales.

The early years of marriage were ideal to Olivia's spiritual way of thinking as she offered in *Rolling Stone*. "We had a nice relationship. When you strive for something higher in the next world, you have a much easier time in this one."

Throughout the 1980's, Olivia would have a front row seat to the often quirky and, by degrees, self-destructive nature of Harrison. Good albums followed by bad albums, legal wrangling centered around A&M Records, Dark Horse and, sometime later Warner Bros. The murder of John Lennon would result in an increased sense of paranoia and fear of the public. The failure of his 1974 tour had so distressed him, that he steadfastly refused many lucrative offers to play live.

Olivia was left to contend with a man who suddenly found himself feeling that what he did was no longer relevant which would send him into periods of emotional withdrawal and self-pity. By this time, Olivia had learned that the best way to deal with her husband and his dark moods was to leave him alone, knowing full well that the only one who could pull Harrison out of his funk was himself.

On a personal front, Olivia would witness a sense of both boredom and professional failure reduce her man to a reclusive homebody who rarely set foot outside of his Friar Park Grounds. With little to do, Harrison soon began to take drugs at a steadily increasing rate while slowly but surely casting aside his long cultivated spiritual and religious beliefs.

But easily the most distressing personal attack on Olivia was that Harrison returned to his cheating days, reportedly having encounters with a number of women while married to Olivia and even in his own home. Years later, Olivia would reveal in *The Guardian* the philosophical and spiritual approach she took in dealing with her husband's infidelities.

"We seemed like partners from the very beginning but our marriage did in fact survive a series of hiccups," said Olivia, using the euphemism 'hiccups' for affairs. "He did like women and women did like him. If he just said a couple of words to you, it would have a profound effect. It was hard to deal with someone who was so well loved."

Olivia had acknowledged that Harrison's affairs were purely physical and, consequently, easier for the couple to overcome. "You go through challenges in your marriage and here is what I found. The first time we had a big hiccup in the road, we came through things and then it was 'Wow!' There is a reward at the end of it. There is an incredible reward because you have lived through more and you have let go of something."

There were sporadic moments in the late 80's when Olivia would once again see the spark in the man she loved. A one off guest appearance in a show by good friend's Jon Lord band *Deep Purple*, something as simple as the recording of an unreleased Bob Dylan song for the soundtrack of a trashy B movie sex romp called *Porky's Revenge* and finally an invitation to join his idol Carl Perkins in an all star live jam. Backstage at the Perkins jam, watching her husband playing and smiling alongside his lifelong idol, brought tears to Olivia's eyes as she remembered in the book *Behind Sad Eyes: The Life of George Harrison.*"That's my old George."

The decade of the 90's started out with good vibrations all around. Olivia had reached out in a myriad of charity good works that included help for Romanian orphans, the Living in a Material World Foundation whose goal it was to sponsor diversity in the arts, all of which were in line with her spiritual thinking and attention to the welfare of children on an international level. In Harrison, she found a willing companion in her good works as the two would often travel the world together, using their influence and contacts to better the world.

For his part, the 90's would see a resurgence for Harrison in both a creative and emotional level. As part of an all star get together called The Traveling Wilburys, which also included such legendary performers as Bob Dylan, Tom Petty, Jeff Lynne and Roy Orbison, offered not only commercial success but an opportunity to return to a long sense of well being and the reason why he got into music in the first place. The association with Lynne would also bring his first taste of real commercial success with the album *Cloud Nine*. Olivia would watch in awe. And no small amount of pride in her man and the love that was in their lives together.

There would be a resurgence in their lives throughout much of the 90's. Harrison would alternate periods of being out and about and musically active with periods of seclusion and contentment. Olivia would look back on that period with a sense of arrival at a period of both love and personal and familial accomplishment all her own. In conversation with *The Telegraph*, she took some credit for the often-noted fact that she was a calming influence on Harrison.

"I gave him a good chance to have a nice home life and a son. If he said I calmed him down, then I probably did calm him down. I used to tell him to cheer down, not cheer up."

But any hope that Olivia and Harrison's life had finally turned for the best and that they would live happily ever after would be dashed in 1997 when Harrison discovered a lump on the back of his neck. In a surprise move, given his attitude of spirituality being a cure all and, no doubt, influenced by Olivia's real world attitude and her notorious eagle eye when it came to monitoring her husband's health, Harrison immediately went to a doctor who determined that the lump was indeed cancerous and was surgically removed. What would not be made public until some years later was that his initial examination had also revealed the early stages of lung cancer and that a part of his lung had also been removed.

For the better part of a year, Harrison remained in seclusion, making the odd appearance at a nearby pub and entertaining a few close friends at the house. That he was appearing frail to those who saw him was considered the result of the surgery. But Olivia could tell that he was once again feeling ill and, at her insistence, Harrison returned to the doctors who examined him and discovered that the cancer had spread to his throat. A massive radiation treatment was successful and it appeared that Harrison was once again on the road to recovery.

Until his world was sent into a traumatic tailspin with the 1999 attack by Michael Abram that left both Olivia and Harrison literally afraid to venture out from their home. Much was made of Olivia's heroic action during the incident but, years later she would set the record straight when she told journalist Katie Couric that there was heroism on all sides.

"George was very brave and people don't know that. He had already been injured and he had to jump up and bring the attacker down to stop him from attacking me. He saved my life too."

Olivia's sense of spirituality and the concept of reincarnation were heightened during this period as both she and Harrison had become highly attuned to the concept of mortality. Harrison would recover both physically and emotionally to the point where he rushed back into what would be a final creative spurt, writing and recording a number of songs that would ultimately see the light as the album *Brainwashed*.

But by early 2001, Harrison was once again feeling ill, which resulted in yet another examination that produced the dire news that Harrison had lung cancer. An operation to remove the cancerous growth from his lung was successful and all seemed right for a time until June, 2001 when Harrison came forward with the news that he had been treated for a brain tumor but was now once again on the mend.

Not surprisingly, Harrison once again became the subject of media frenzy and speculation. Fans began gathering at Harrison's house, chanting 'Hare Krishna' and "My Sweet Lord" and voicing their hopes and prayers for him. There would also be a story that surfaced that said Harrison had confided in a close friend that he was near death, a story that Harrison and Olivia were quick to dismiss as "unsubstantiated, untrue, insensitive and uncalled for."

However, a story published by *BBC News* that excerpted liberally from an interview Olivia would do with journalist Katie Couric, indicated that, in a spiritual sense, Harrison was already preparing for the end. "He gave his life to God a long time ago. He wasn't trying to hang onto anything. He was fine with it. He went with what was happening."

Harrison would make sporadic appearances into late 2001, an unannounced gig at a local pub, the occasional charity event appearance and what would be his last studio work, laying down some guitar licks for albums by Bill Wyman and Jim Capaldi. But the consensus that Harrison's days were numbered were confirmed in November 2001 when his cancer returned with a vengeance and laid waste to his already weakened body. With Olivia and Dhani, Harrison went from hospital to hospital in a last ditch attempt at a cure that, sadly, would not come. In his weakened state, Harrison met with his longtime Beatle brothers McCartney and Starr in what was described as an emotional last chat that was tearful and, to the end, punctuated by Harrison's sarcastic sense of humor.

Olivia would remember that moment and others years later in conversation with *The Sunday Times*. "George was the funniest man I knew. When he died, it was like 'Oh no, the party's over.' He didn't put up with any crabbiness other than his own."

By late November, Harrison was ready to go to God. George Harrison passed away on November 29, 2001 at 1:30 p.m. Olivia would recall Harrison's last words in *The Telegraph*. "He told me 'Olivia you'll be fine,'" she reflected. "For me, fine was okay but it was not really good enough. I am fine and I am okay. He walked his road and now I have to walk mine. There's no way of going around grief. I think it's better to just go through it."

And while there would be tears and moments of loneliness in Olivia's life with Harrison's passing, there would always be a sense of belief that would see her through. "There's no dying of the light," she told *The Independent*. "I feel very fortunate. I have a lot of joy because I know it's okay. The physical world is not the end by any means. It's just another place you pass through. I don't just believe that. I know it."

Olivia's sadness was palpable and she would spend a number of years in seclusion, venturing out into the public only for occasional charitable situations connected to Harrison's life and legacy, the completion and release, with the help of her son Dhani, of Harrison's final album *Brainwashed* and becoming the legacy and economic gatekeeper of Harrison's interest in all things Beatles. Personally, there continued to be the longing for her lost love.

One element of her pain and sadness manifested itself in the fact that, some years after Harrison's death, she continued to wear her wedding ring. "I still like to put on my wedding ring every morning and just look at it," she told *The Telegraph*. But, with the years, the realist mixed with her spiritual side in Olivia was seemingly never far from her thoughts as she contemplated her years with Harrison and what it was now be like without him.

"I am still having a relationship with him but it is not a physical relationship anymore. If you have ever had anybody go who you have loved, you do feel in communication with them because you feel so deeply in your heart that if you say a prayer it goes straight to them."

The ensuing years have seen a gradual evolution in Olivia.

Out of necessity, she has gone from being quite happy out of the limelight to being a selective but often enthusiastic spokesperson when it came to promoting anything connected to her late husband. And on that front, she has been quite busy. Over the years, she has supervised the re-releasing of Harrison's solo work in various configurations. She wrote a heartfelt introduction to a later edition of Harrison's autobiography *I, Me, Mine*. Olivia has overcome what many perceived as shyness to be a guest at a number of events related to the commemoration of Harrison and/or The Beatles. Her relationship with former Beatle wives has been good and, in a giant step both professionally and personally, she served as co-producer on the Martin Scorsese documentary *George Harrison: Living in a Material World*. It also goes without saying that she has contributed and worked tirelessly for countless charities.

Now well into her 70's, Olivia is living a life of contentment, surrounded by her memories of Harrison and the productive, spiritually driven life she has created for herself. But it is a life that, to many observers, is not complete.

Her life has been devoid of love and romance since the death of her husband and one wonders if, at this late stage, there is still the possibility of falling in love. On the rare occasion when that question has been broached, she has been quick with a laugh and an Olivia style dance around it.

"I don't have time for that. I still have so much work to do."

Chapter Eight
Heather Mills/McCartney

How does the old saying go? Truth is stranger than fiction? As it pertains to Heather Mills/McCartney, the answer might well be that truth and fiction are equally strange. Because the life and times of the former wife of Paul McCartney are literally one never ending trip down the rabbit hole to Wonderland where everything is immediately in doubt but, upon further examination, there just might be a shred of something to it.

But whatever your level of belief or disbelief may be, one thing is certain, you'd have to go all the way back to Yoko Ono to find a Beatle wife who was more universally, disliked, disbelieved and, to a large extent, is deserving of being so universally maligned by just about everything she has done or said since day one of her existence. Alternately dubbed a liar, a thief, a gold digger, a publicity hound and just an all around not nice person, the story of Heather Mills/McCartney is the tale of a moving target who has often been the one to pull the trigger.

In all fairness, Heather has not always come across as a loose cannon and, as she exhibited in conversation with *US Magazine*, could be quite even keel about the demise of her relationship with McCartney. "This is someone I fell in love with. To me, he was a normal guy who happened to write a few cool songs in the 60's and the 70's. You fall in love, you get married and then sometimes you go 'Oh my God! This is completely wrong.' Then you wake up and you move on."

However, as plain spoken as Heather could be, the outrageous side of Heather has never seemed too far from the surface, as when she was excerpted in *UltimateClassicRock.com* as blasting the media that constantly attacked her. "I've had more worse press than a pedophile and a murderer."

Admittedly, Heather's life and times are marked by outrageous statements that often walk the line between fact and fabrication and have often been challenged and disproved. But bottom line, her life is her life as she sees it.

Heather Ann Mills was born in England on January 12, 1968, the first of what would be three children born to John and Beatrice Mills. It was reportedly a happy occasion when Heather was born and cynics would acknowledge that her birth may well have been the last good thing that happened to her. Heather's childhood was chaotic to say the least, surrounded as she was by seemingly endless violence and chaos on the part of her parents.

"I didn't have a happy childhood," she told *The Guardian*. "My dad was very abusive and very violent. I watched him being violent to my mother for so long that I felt relief for her when she finally ran away and left us all when I was nine. I thought I don't have to watch her get beaten up and thrown through windows anymore."

But along the bumpy road that would be her childhood, Heather would find small pockets in solace in the fact that she did discover certain traits that would follow her in later life. "My father was an ex army paratrooper who behaved like a general." She offered in *The Guardian*. "So my discipline, focus and belief that I can do anything in sport came from him. We were encouraged to do any kind of sport. We'd get up in the morning and swim 200 lengths in the pool and before walking four miles to school. My mother wasn't very communicative. I remember her giving us only one kiss in my entire life. But she was a brilliant speaker and a deep thinker."

At age eight, Heather has said that she and a friend were kidnapped and sexually assaulted by a swim coach who, would allegedly commit suicide after the alleged deed was discovered and the truth of it would be the first of countless Heather stories to be endlessly debated. Life with her father was rapidly disintegrating around Heather and her siblings according to Heather's autobiography entitled *A Single Step*. There never seemed to be enough money in their house and their father insisted that the children go out and shoplift food and clothing. The situation became more dire when, about the time Heather turned 15, her father was convicted of fraud and sentenced to 18 months in prison, leaving the three children essentially on their own.

Heather recalled in an *ABC News* interview that, during that period, she became the de facto parent to her two younger siblings. "From a very young age I had to cook and clean and steal clothes and steal food."

Heather and her sister Fiona would go to live for a time with her long since departed mother who had, by that time, taken up with an actor named Charles Stapley. It was an uneasy situation according to Stapley in an interview years later with *The London Evening Standard*. "I felt dreadfully sorry for her when she came to live with us. All she ever wanted to do was to make something of herself and to escape her past."

After a time, Heather and her sister would return to living with her father, only to find that the violence and dysfunction would continue. "One minute my father would be all sweetness and light and the next he would be like Attila the Hun," Heather told the *New York Post*. "He thought nothing of throwing us down the stairs."

The last straw for Heather was slow in coming but, when it did, it was nothing if not final.

By age 15, Heather had had enough and ran away from home to work in a travelling carnival, where she had the first of many complicated relationships when she fell in love with a carnival worker named Peter who would tragically die of a heroin overdose not long after he and Heather met. Destitute and homeless, Heather lived for a time in a cardboard box under the arches of London's Waterloo Bridge. She would ruefully describe that situation in her book *A Single Step* when she offered, "I was living cold and stiff inside my Pamper's box."

And, as she would recall in an *AOL interview*, missing out on all the normal teenage rites of passage, including, ironically, the heyday of The Beatles was almost an afterthought. "I was too busy surviving and getting on with my life to be a fan of anybody. I was never a Beatles fan."

When she could find them, Heather would manage a series of jobs that inevitably resulted in her being fired or quitting. Working for a jewelry store would result in a first criminal conviction when she was caught stealing a number of gold chains from the store. She would be found guilty as charged but, most likely, because of her age, was put on probation.

Heather continued on her downward spiral until, at age 17, she met Alfie Karmal, a European entrepreneur who convinced her that she had what it took to be a successful model. Heather was intrigued rather than suspicious and readily accepted the suggestion. It would be a pivotal point in Heather's life. It turned out that, in looks and attitude, she was, indeed, model quality and would begin modeling swimwear and fashionable clothing in runway shows, showrooms and catalogues. She was making money, doing a bit of traveling and rubbing shoulders with a level of style and upper class society that she had never experienced before.

Her relationship with Karmal remained friendly and professional but it soon became evident that things between Heather and the much older Karmal were heating up which might well have been the reason that in 1987, while on a modeling assignment in Paris, she became the mistress of a European businessman named George Kazan, a relationship that would last two years and would result in her most notable contribution to her modeling resume, shooting a nude photo session for a German sex education manual called *The Joys of Love.*

By the time her relationship with Kazan had run its course, Heather was feeling the need to settle down and start a family. It was a deep seeded desire, born of a childhood that had seen her life wrapped in dysfunction as she explained in *The Guardian.* "My parents' relationship made me want to make that family unit that I never really had. Because of that, it made me want to marry very young."

Upon returning to London, Heather made the very forward move for her time of proposing marriage to Karmal, the much older man with children from a previous relationship whom Heather considered her first proper boyfriend. Karmal agreed to the proposal under one condition. She had to do something about her compulsive lying which had become a daily part of his and Heather's relationship.

Heather agreed and would spend the next eight weeks with a psychiatrist, digging deep into a psyche that had been conditioned to lie by her father. Heather emerged from the therapy, assuring Karmal that she knew why she lied and would do everything humanly possible to stop. Karmal was satisfied and the couple married in 1989.

The next three years would be an emotional rollercoaster for both parties. Two ectopic pregnancies, Heather's alleged continued lying and rumors that she had gone from wanting a stable marriage to being a party girl for Arab royalty, ended in divorce when Heather reportedly fell in love with a ski instructor while on holiday.

The ink had barely dried on her divorce papers to Karmal when Heather had already ditched the ski instructor in favor of yet another beau, a wealthy banker named Raffaele Mincione. It was while on holiday in the middle east in 1992 that the war in Croatia broke out and, at that moment, Heather was hit hard by the plight of refugees caught in the middle of the conflict and her self-centered nature immediately morphed into that of a philanthropist.

Over the next two years, Heather would use her growing influence in high society to form a refugee center in London that would, according to reports, get more than 20 refugees out of the line of fire and into a safer life. During this period, she would fund her philanthropic efforts by taking modeling assignments in Australia and would often find herself literally in the middle of the conflict, driving through war torn land to deliver donations to the needy.

By the time the dust settled in 1993, her charity work at the front lines had seemingly turned her life for the better. Heather suddenly had goals and, by degrees, had become a woman of substance. But all that would change on August 8, 1993. Heather and Mincione were walking down a London street. They were on their way to a nearby park where, unbeknownst to Mincione, Heather was about to break the news to him that their relationship was over.

In an interview with *CNN's* Larry King, Heather recalled what happened next. "I heard two police cars go flying by. I sort of took a step and then another step after those police cars went by. And then a police motor bike came out of nowhere and chopped my leg off, crushed my pelvis, punctured my lung and split my head open." She lay in the street, a bloody witness to her carnage as she related to *ABC News*. "The cars were going around the leg and there was blood everywhere. I was just lying there in the middle of the street, watching my leg and thinking 'What on earth is my leg doing over there?'"

Heather would spend some time in the hospital, miraculously surviving the ordeal but at the expense of the loss of her leg six inches below her knee. She described the emotional turmoil to the *New York Daily News*. "When I woke in the hospital and was told that I had lost my leg, it was traumatic. There were times when I was really unhappy. But after a time, I knew I could cope and I knew that everything would be alright." She continued to look inward during her recovery as she offered to *ABC News*. "I knew this was happening for a reason and that somehow [I can use what happened to me] to make a difference."

But before she could make a difference, Heather's mind instinctively turned to making a buck. A settlement with the London Police Department over the accident netted Heather an estimated $200 thousand pounds. She sold the rights to her accident and her early life to the tabloid

News of The World for a tidy amount and put the money into her philanthropic efforts, setting up the Heather Mills Health Trust for the purpose of delivering prosthetic limbs to people who had lost limbs after stepping on landmines. She would also use her growing notoriety to become a spokesperson for the organization Adopt a Minefield, a United Nations campaign dedicated to clearing minefields left after the conclusion of wars. In 1995, Heather would capitalize on the increased interest in her life by publishing an autobiography called *Out on a Limb* (which would be released some years later under the title *A Single Step*) in which she revealed her inspirational comeback from the accident as well as revealing, for the first time, the details of her dysfunctional early years.

While she was quite serious in her philanthropic efforts, the late 90's also saw her plunging headlong into a number of romantic relationships that would once again add fuel to her flighty/imaginative nature.

In 1995, she was briefly engaged to media executive Marcus Stapleton after knowing him for only 16 days. As reported in *The London Times* and *The Daily Telegraph*, Heather was romantically involved with documentary filmmaker Chris Terrill. Things went bad in that relationship fairly quickly as Heather unexpectedly called off their engagement five days before the couple's planned wedding day as Heather charged that Terrill was gay, a secret MI6 spy and had been assigned to secretly sabotage her anti-mine work. For his part, Terrill would tell *The Daily Telegraph* that "I soon realized that Heather had a somewhat elastic relationship with the truth, which she was able to stretch impressively at times."

Through 1999, Heather remained emotionally and, perhaps, psychologically all over the place but anchored by a busy schedule of good works. She was very much on her own. As was a musician named Paul McCartney.

McCartney, less than a year removed from burying the true love of his life, Linda, was lonely and in a very vulnerable state. Like two ships passing in the night, McCartney and Heather would first lay eyes on each other during a charity awards event in which both were presenters.

"I saw her at an awards ceremony but we didn't meet," McCartney was quoted in an *ABC News* story. "I just heard her speak and I thought she was pretty impressive."

What Heather would quickly discover was that besides being

impressed, McCartney was also mesmerized by what he would discover was her quick and subtle wit, that she could be quite opinionated and down to earth. Most would be quick to dismiss the notion that there was a lot of Linda's forthrightness and sincerity in Heather. But in McCartney's still fragile emotional state, maybe the comparison was valid.

Whatever the case, McCartney was suddenly very conspicuous in Heather's world. He made a generous donation to Heather's anti-mine charity and, when Heather and her sister Fiona conceived a charity driven song to further her causes, McCartney made what many considered the serious move of sitting in on the song's recording and offering backup vocals.

Heather, in a quote from the *SF Gate*, saw the gestures as part and parcel of McCartney's interest in her. "He pursued me for months. It was very flattering. How could you say no [to that attention]?"

As it would turn out, Heather, within their first week of dating, cut to the chase. McCartney was known for being big on large families and Heather had been told on several occasions that, given the damage done by her previous ectopic pregnancies, she would probably never be able to have children. "I told him within the first week of dating that I would not be able to get pregnant," she told *CNN* host Larry King. "I was very open about it. I told him 'If you're not interested than off you go.'"

But McCartney was interested and, as they became more of a public couple, so were the press. In the beginning, Heather and McCartney had decided to remain silent on the press inquiries but that did not stop the media, especially the shadier tabloid press, from wild speculation that included not too veiled speculation that Heather was after McCartney for his wealth and prestige. To her credit, Heather displayed a fairly thick skin, laughing off the more outrageous headlines and keeping her private life just that.

"I was always in the press before I met Paul," she said to *CNN*. "So I wasn't one of those unlucky people that just sort of came into the limelight and suddenly nasty things were being written. The public aren't stupid. But they presume that, because there are so many Beatle fans, Paul fans, everyone is kind of going to hate me."

During their courtship, Heather would see a side of McCartney that had always been hinted at but had rarely been seen by those outside his inner circle. She told *ABC News* that, in those early days of their relationship, she found McCartney to "be very creative, artistic and flighty. He brings out the child in me." Years later, Heather would grow nostalgic at the memory of those early days as she reflected to *BBC* host Michael Parkinson. "He's very romantic, that's why I fell in love with him. Romance to me is not just writing a check. Romance to me is picking up a feather. It's bringing me breakfast in bed no matter how he feels. It's that kind of thoughtfulness."

And it was that sense of thoughtfulness and romance that surprised Heather in July 2001 when on holiday in the Lake District, just north of London, that McCartney dropped to one knee. "I thought someone had shot him in the back of his kneecaps because he just all of a sudden fell to the ground," she chuckled in an *ABC News* interview. "I gasped and asked him if he was all right? He said 'I love you. Will you marry me?'"

Of course, anything or anyone connected to the Beatles or a former Beatle was instant news all over the world and, as was often the case in the media frenzy that inevitably followed, a press conference was called within a matter of days to announce the happy event.

For McCartney, answering softball questions and bobbing and weaving in the glare of a photographer's camera flash, was pretty much old hat. But despite also having a history of dealing with the press, Heather was a bit awestruck by this bit of nostalgic Beatlemania. But she good-naturedly went along with the inane and obvious questions. How she felt when McCartney proposed was an easy one. "I was in shock," she said in a news report filed by the *BBC*. "I was over the moon. But at one point, the rebellious, contrary side of Heather emerged when the gaggle of photographers aggressively screamed for the couple to kiss for the cameras. "We don't kiss on demand," chuckled Heather. "It has to be spontaneous." When she was asked if she would take McCartney's last name after they were married, Heather would be equally defiant when she offered, "I won't be using the title Lady. I'm not into all that pretense."

There was only one potential pitfall to this storybook relationship. McCartney's children were immediately leery of their father falling in love so quickly after the death of Linda and, like the public at large, were suspicious of Heather latching onto their father for financial rewards and status rather than love. Heather was quick to get the picture and cooled everybody's suspicions when she readily agreed to sign a prenuptial agreement but McCartney would reject the offer. But Heather went to further lengths to prove that she was not the gold digger she was being portrayed as when she offered to draw up her own agreement that would protect her husband's fortune. "I wanted to prove that I loved him for him," she would tell *Vanity Fair*.

Heather and McCartney were married on June 11, 2002 at Castle Leslie in Ireland. By comparison to previous Beatle marriages, the nuptials for Heather and McCartney were a rather elaborate affair that included a McCartney song entitled *"Heather"* playing romantically during the ceremony. Heather was in bliss following the wedding as she and McCartney settled into the first year of their marriage.

"I fell in love with him after he had chased me for a while," she opined to *CNN* host Parkinson. "He was very charming and wooing. He is a fantastic man." But she also acknowledged in the same conversation that she had not entered into the relationship blindly. "But the stuff that comes with it [the marriage] is very hard to deal with."

And how she dealt with 'the stuff,' the constant intrusion and badgering of a press that was becoming more aggressive as it pertained to all things McCartney and, now, herself was to go completely the other way. "After eight years of being very open and available to the press, I decided to go quiet," she told *CNN*. "I wanted to protect Paul and his children and their privacy because they were very private people."

Unfortunately, Heather's silence would result in the press launching, to her way of thinking, a wave of totally made up stories that not only affected her charity work but her personal life as well. Stories continued to play up the continued adversarial relationship between Heather and the McCartney children, reported financial improprieties when it came to her charity work and, in perhaps the most hurtful cut of all, a story that claimed Heather had had a miscarriage during her first year of marriage to McCartney. Heather would be hurt and disappointed at what she perceived as the lies being printed but, instead, turned to the positive side of her marriage.

From all reports, it appeared that marriage had a soothing effect on Heather. She could regularly be found cooking vegetarian based meals for McCartney and his family. She weaned herself off an addiction to chocolate candy and would often marvel at how McCartney, often known as the messy Beatle during his wild single days, was now a cleaning machine, going to great lengths to make sure the house was spotless. Her time with her stepchildren, tabloid reports aside, appeared to be ideal.

Heather was also finding time to spread her wings both charitably and professionally, continuing to be a spokesperson for her anti-minefield and artificial limbs campaigns while growing into a reliable spokeswoman for both the vegetarian and animal rights movements.

By degrees she would eventually come around to doing a bit of press every once in a while and would be quite candid when dealing with friendly interrogators like Larry King and Michael Parkinson. And McCartney was quick to acknowledge that Heather's presence in his life had been inspiring as he succinctly put it in an *Interview* conversation. "Being in love with her makes me want to write songs."

But while everything was rosy on the surface, what would remain unsettled and unsaid was the fact that Heather did not seem able to conceive. McCartney remained magnanimous in his support for Heather's issue and was quite content to have her be a very good stepmother to his children. But one day, everything changed in their lives as Heather recalled in a conversation with *CNN*.

"I went to the hospital for some general tests and, as it turned out, that was when I didn't have my monthly cycle. I had done the pregnancy test and it came up positive. When I got home, I immediately went upstairs where Paul was in a meeting. I kept walking in and out of the meeting and I kept saying 'are you finished yet?' He kept looking at me like my behavior wasn't normal. At one point, he came out of the meeting and I showed him the test results. We both started crying."

Beatrice McCartney was born on October 28, 2003. Heather and McCartney were over the moon with happiness. But the happiness would be tempered by the fact that the UK press had taken umbrage with Heather continuing to not talk to them and, thus, had taken to a nearly nonstop barrage of what she perceived as false stories about McCartney and herself that touched on the notion that their marriage was, reportedly, a marriage in crisis thanks to Heather's domineering attitude toward her husband. In her darkest moments, Heather, as reported by *ABC News*, would acknowledge that she often fantasized about a different kind of life.

"I would like nothing more than to live a more anonymous life," she declared. "If the press keeps attacking me, I might just have to be a stay at home wife. If I did that, my life would be a lot easier."

An attack that particularly irked Heather was the charge that she had turned McCartney into a henpecked husband. It was a charge that upon further examination seemed to have a kernel of truth to it. McCartney had conceded in *ABC News* and elsewhere, often with tongue firmly planted in cheek, that Heather could be quite bossy and overbearing because she was so single minded. Heather, in somewhat of a backhanded defense of McCartney's statements, said in *ABC News*. "This is a man who has had his own way his entire life. It's sometimes hard to listen to other people's opinions. I'm very opinionated and so is he. But men need to be bossed."

By 2005, the daily emotional and mental conflict was wreaking havoc with McCartney and Heather's personal lives as she sighed in conversation with *ABC News*. "We ended up spending day after day explaining and having to justify ourselves to the British tabloids. Last year was horrendous publicly. It was probably the worst year of my life."

The stress of public scrutiny had begun to take its toll. By the end of 2005, Heather and McCartney were reportedly living apart and although they would occasionally be spotted together at various events, their 'togetherness' was coming across as forced. The consensus among the attacking tabloid press was that their marriage was truly on the rocks. The barrage of headlines, a mixture of speculation and half-truths, finally became a reality on May 17, 2006 when Heather and McCartney announced their separation.

In excerpts from their announcement, reported by *The Guardian* and a literal army of tabloid and mainstream press, the couple, in a dual statement said "Our parting is amicable and we still care about each other very much. But we have found it increasingly difficult to maintain a normal relationship with the constant intrusion on our private lives. Separation for any couple is difficult enough but to have to go through this so publicly is immensely stressful."

In the aftermath of the announcement, Heather was emotionally at cross-purposes, alternately sad, angry, withdrawn, reflective and, by turns, defiant and philosophical. And in an interview with *Event Magazine*, in the aftermath of what would be a prolonged, two-year odyssey to divorce, Heather was many of those things.

"Losing my leg was easier to cope with than divorce. For some reason, it's very hard to be married to a Beatle. I say what I think. If I think something is wrong, I will say it. If I wasn't that type of person we'd still be married now. For years, I was attracted to these very strong, powerful men who thought they wanted a strong woman but actually they wanted someone who did what they wanted."

Heather was much less reflective as the divorce proceedings commenced and had reverted to the negativity and attacking, often outrageous attitude that had followed her since childhood. Money was suddenly becoming an issue to Heather. She was making support demands in the neighborhood of 125 million pounds while McCartney was offering a shade over 15 million pounds. Heather would claim that she had gone so far as to hire a private accounting firm to investigate McCartney's financial holdings. That's when things started getting personal.

In an interview with *Extra*, Heather unloaded on McCartney's daughter Stella. "Every single week, Stella tried to break up our marriage. She was afraid I would get all the planes and diamonds. I can't protect her any longer. She's done evil, evil things." At one point in the proceedings, court documents were leaked to *The Daily Telegraph* and countless media outlets in which Heather stated that McCartney was often drunk, smoked marijuana, stabbed her with a broken wine glass, pushed her over a table and pushed her into a bathtub while she was pregnant. Needless to say, the public perception was that Heather was not creditable at best and out of control and lying at worst.

If public opinion was any indication, the six days of divorce hearings in February 2008 were a mere formality. McCartney came across as calm and believable while Heather, who at one point had gone so far as to fire her attorney and represent herself, was out of control and contradictory. In the end, a legal divorce was granted with Heather receiving 16.5 million pounds, ownership of one residence and 35,000 pounds annually for child support and schooling.

The divorce was over but, for Heather, the next years would be a constant battle.

With the divorce, Heather was now like blood in the water for the ravenous tabloid press who viewed her divorce as carte blanche to continue their attacks. At one point, it was estimated that the tabloids had printed more than 4400 negative articles about her. Heather would launch lawsuits against several of the more notorious newspapers to seemingly no avail, although at some point there would be several halfhearted apologies from the tabloids. Heather seemed to be thrashing around in a world that she helped create.

But she would continue her involvement in several charity causes and by 2009, she remained a precarious pop culture icon, seemingly using every opportunity to generate press and be relevant. It was almost as if her marriage to McCartney had dissolved into almost an afterthought and that the real culprit remained Heather herself, an emotional dervish casting out controversy wherever she went. The controversies would continue to follow her, at one point she was named by the magazine *Marketing* as one of the top five most hated female celebrities in the world.

But in her own often outrageous and self-destructive way, Heather would be resilient, using her own out of control persona and the fact that she was now the ex-wife of a Beatle (which she quickly discovered had its own bit of cache) to her advantage as she explored a myriad of opportunities that revolved around her vegan lifestyle.

She opened a vegan restaurant called VBites that would have a quite successful run before shuttering its doors in 2017. In line with that Heather bought out a food production company rechristened it VBites Foods. She would also launch a 55-acre storage and business space exclusively for vegan businesses called Vegan Enterprises. Needless to say, Heather was much in demand as a motivational speaker and spokesperson for the vegan lifestyle.

Her charitable works would also continue as a constant spokesperson and advocate for Adopt a Minefield and organizations supporting prosthetic limbs for victims of war, animal rights and other organizations.

But it would not be all work and no play.

Always looking for a way to capitalize on her notoriety, Heather caught the tidal wave of cheesy reality competition television shows with appearances on *Dancing with the Stars* and *Dancing on Ice*. Heather would also maintain a bit of a jet setting lifestyle, traveling the world and hanging with the upper crust. And while the inevitable specter of ex-Beatle wife still sat on her shoulders, it was becoming less an entryway into polite society as Heather's rejuvenated and, yes, sometimes outrageous personality made her somebody A listers wanted to hang out with.

In the best possible way, Heather was finally free and, as exhibited in the likes of *ZeeNews.com* and *ContactMusic.com*, she was often willing to talk about it. "I'm really having a great time. It's great freedom. I get asked out all the time and my girlfriends always want to know why. Maybe because, now, I'm comfortable with myself."

To the extent that she has been quite forward in anything

approaching a serious relationship. She matter-of-factly recalled a post-divorce relationship with a DJ that lasted six years. And then there was the time she passed a very young looking filmmaker on a train and slipped him a note saying "I think you're hot" along with information on how to contact her. That would lead to a relationship that lasted a number of years and appeared headed for the altar before they went their separate ways. In that regard, Heather told the *Press & Journal* that, in no certain terms, would she ever say 'I do' again.

"I'm very open to falling in love. But I'd never get married again. In my mind, that's nothing more than a legal document that causes a lot of hassles. Besides, I'm looking for someone who can match me and my friends say there's no such person on the planet."

Heather offers that she is not obsessing about what has been the high and low points in her life and what maybe in her future. She has come through her life and the Beatles wife experience and remains bloodied, unbowed and a woman whose personal philosophy on life has allowed her to overcome a lot and that allows her to live for a future that will always be just around the corner and a past that will always be looking over her shoulder.

"I'm not bitter about that time [with McCartney]. What would be the point? The level of personal abuse forced me to retreat from my public profile and allowed me to look at my life anew, to find myself new challenges and to get more balance in my lifestyle. In a way it turned out to be a gift."

A gift that allows Heather to awaken each day without the fear of seeing her name in a tabloid headline. "I just go with the flow these days and feel truly happy and lucky," she told the *Press & Journal*. "If I died tomorrow, I'd be content that I've already ticked every box of what I wanted to achieve. My aim now is to go to my grave knowing I used every aspect of myself.

I may go out battered and bruised but I'll feel like I've lived my life."

Chapter Nine
Nancy Shevell/McCartney

It seems that Paul McCartney would either never learn or is scared to death of being alone even for a minute. In 2007, with his marriage to Heather essentially over but still almost a year away from ending in divorce, McCartney was already once again involved.

Enter Nancy Shevell.

Nancy is an enigma of sorts when it comes to former and current spouses of the Beatles. And the reality is easily spelled out. American. Jewish, high-class, comes from money and has money, has functioned quite well in the business world. More akin to McCartney's first wife, Linda, than any of the other Beatle wives. There's a quiet sense of style, elegance and grace about her. When she walks into a room, everybody notices in the best possible way. But the thing that must have been most attractive to McCartney was her desire to stay below the radar and as far from the public eye as possible.

Nancy has rarely given interviews, so rarely in fact that a pre-McCartney interview with the *Newark News Ledger* newspaper is alleged to be the only interview of any length she has ever given in her life. And to say that she is publicity shy is an understatement. She has always been averse to having her picture taken, especially with people she did not know. Famed television celebrity journalist Barbara Walters, Nancy's second cousin, echoed those sentiments when she told *The Observer,* "Nancy has never gotten used to the attention. She has never wanted anything to do with publicity. She once turned down a chance to do a big piece in *Vogue.*"

But being publicity shy was not the only thing that made Nancy and McCartney prime candidates for a love match. With Nancy there was always a sense of propriety and, yes, breeding that made her a deft combination of sophistication and down to earth humanity that came natural and easy for somebody who was entering the highly charged, celebrity world of McCartney.

Popeater.com reporter Rob Shuter painted the perfect picture of Nancy when he offered, "Shevell comes with all the skills that Linda had to learn and that Heather never learned. Nancy is not as bubbly or full of life as Heather was but she comes with fewer problems." *The London Evening Standard* would echo those attributes in a headline that described Nancy as "Elegant, publicity shy and oh so discreet."

Discreet to the point that when she was asked by *The Observer* to talk about herself, she said "I'm over 50. I work. That's it. There really isn't that much to talk about."

Well before Nancy came into the world, the name Shevell was known for being hardworking, industrious and, occasionally, dancing on the wrong side of the law. During the 1920's, Myron Shevell made a living as the head of a small but thriving truck transportation company that ran seafood on a fairly short run from New Jersey to New York. By this time, Myron had settled down to a slightly upper class lifestyle in Edison, New Jersey with his wife Arlene and, on November 20, 1959, their second child, Nancy Shevell was born.

By the 60's Myron and his brother Daniel had formed their own company called *New* England Motor Freight. The brothers Shevell were hardcore businessmen who would often cut legal corners as their business grew, which, in turn, led to some under the table dealings with some unsavory types. In 1975, New England Motor Freight was investigated by the federal authorities and charged with fraud and not too veiled charges of doing business with the Mafia. The case against the Shevell's would never go to trial but the brothers were forced to surrender control of their company and subsequently declared bankruptcy. Daniel Shevell, despondent over the charges, would commit suicide that same year.

Myron was making a go of it business wise but, by 1988, had succumbed to temptation and had once again fallen in with the wrong crowd. Shortly after reemerging with yet another transportation company, Myron was once again charged with fraud and more Mafia dealings when it was alleged that he made illegal payoffs to mob types in exchange for allowing his new venture to dodge certain union rules. Once again, this case did not go to trial but Myron was barred from being involved in any union negotiations for five years.

How witnessing her father's legal and business entanglements at a fairly young age had molded Nancy's attitude toward being in the public eye is not certain. But what she would readily admit in conversation with the *Newark News Ledger* was that growing up in a world of trucks and truckers was entertaining in a different sort of way. "I loved it when my father brought me toy trucks as gifts. I used to line them up in my room right next to my Barbies. While other kids would go feed the ducks in the park, I would go to my father's truck terminals every single weekend."

Nancy grew up in relative luxury and, even as a child and into her early teens, was coming together as a quiet, confident, poised and straightforward young woman. But that did not stop her from having a wild array of influences on her life. She loved skiing and flying and could be a bit of a tomboy. Nancy was an inveterate reader and could be counted on to explore such literary outliers as Charles Bukowski and such pop culture icons as Robin Williams. It went without saying that her parents and, in particular, her father's business acumen, was rubbing off on her.

Her years at John P. Stevens High School were not widely reported but it has been noted that she was very sports' oriented and athletic, participating in the school's all-girl football program and was a solid soccer player. How good a student she was remains a bit of a mystery but the fact that she would graduate with good enough grades to matriculate to *Arizona State University* and, to the surprise of many, get a degree in transportation, then an unusual occurrence for a woman in the normally male-dominated occupation, spoke volumes about her drive and tenacity.

Along the way, Nancy would find time to fall in love.

Nancy was in love with this smooth, good looking and leaning heavily Republican Bruce Blakeman. The impression was that, besides pushing for a law degree, he was somebody who harbored political ambitions. And to do that, close, unnamed observers of the relationship recalled in a *New York Daily News*, he was looking for his societal and financial future and saw Nancy as the ideal package for those goals. But again, for Nancy it was all about being young and in love. They would soon marry and, in short order, Nancy would be pregnant with the couple's child, a boy named Arlen.

Following her graduation from Arizona State, Nancy would slide effortlessly into the family business. She would go to work for The Shevell Group of Companies in 1983. And true to her nature, her drive, ambition and low-key attention to detail and the bottom line soon overrode any hint of nepotism among her fellow workers. So much so that nary an eyebrow was raised in 1986 when she was named as Vice President of the corporation. During this period, she became well known as somebody who could hold her own in any business dealings. In the aftermath of one particularly heated confrontation with a colleague, she would comment to *The Star Ledger* "I don't know where he is now but I know where I am."

Nancy's political connections would result in her being appointed by then New York Governor George Pataki to the board of the Metropolitan Transit Authority, an unpaid position she would hold for more than a decade.

As the couple began to move up in their respective careers, they rented a weekend home in the high end of the Hamptons. It was in the late 80's that they became friends with McCartney and his then wife Linda. Nancy and Linda developed a very strong tie during this period, one based on both being Jewish and a similar, down to earth attitude. With Linda's death, McCartney and Nancy would maintain a good social relationship.

Nancy felt comfortable enough that she could be straight up with her opinions. In the following years, her candor would put a strain on their relationship. McCartney began dating Heather not long after Linda's death and would often bring her around the Hamptons for a visit. On one occasion, McCartney and Nancy were talking when she backhandedly offered a critique of Heather when she said, in a *London Evening Standard* article, that he didn't have to marry every woman he dated. From all accounts, McCartney, who by that time was more than a bit smitten with Heather, took her comments badly and the pair cooled their relationship for a period of time.

In 1996, Nancy discovered that she had breast cancer. Getting on in years and with a history of cancer in her family with her mother having succumbed to the disease some years earlier, she nevertheless used her innate toughness and determination to get through a year of worry and tests before it was determined that she was now cancer free.

As the years passed, it was becoming obvious to those in her inner circle and, most likely to Bruce and Nancy, that their marriage, while not completely on the rocks, was in a downward spiral according to a detailed investigation by the *New York Daily News*. Unnamed sources in the story recalled that the marriage was marked by a constant clash of egos. Nancy, according to insiders, had a sense of entitlement while Bruce, juggling a law career and high hopes for a political future, was driven by fame, notoriety and recognition. Which meant that a lot of their free time was spent going to political functions and various benefits that Nancy did not want any part of and would often end up home alone while Bruce went alone. Consequently, the couple was spending a lot of time apart, often working in different states. As the marriage spiraled down in the mid 2000's, they would finally separate.

It was about that time that McCartney and Heather were, likewise, separated after four often rancorous years of marriage. Given his nature, it was not surprising that, well before the divorce would be final, McCartney was already back on the dating scene with a vengeance. "What can I say?" McCartney would tell *The Guardian*. "I just like being in love."

But there was more to McCartney at this point than sheer emotion and loneliness. Still recovering from the aftermath of his marriage to Heather and the notion that she may well have been in love with his money and fame rather than him, McCartney was now looking for something different in a woman, somebody well established in her life and her profession, somebody who had her own level of wealth and, perhaps most importantly, somebody for whom money wasn't such a big deal.

Between March and November of 2007, McCartney would be romantically linked to actresses Rosanna Arquette, Reneé Zellweger and models Elle Macpherson and Christie Brinkley. Nancy was well aware that McCartney was available and truth be known, in the wake of her separation from her husband and adjusting quite admirably to once again being single after all these years, was somewhat interested in getting to know McCartney a bit better. But given her high society upbringing and shy demeanor, she may well have been at a loss as to how to attract his attention.

Enter Barbara Walters, noted celebrity journalist/interviewer, a co-host of the television series *The View* and, most importantly, Nancy's second cousin and close personal friend. Over the years, Nancy had found Walters an emotional confidant and, when she would confide in her about an interest in McCartney, Walters stepped in and played matchmaker. She began throwing dinner parties with McCartney in mind, inviting people that McCartney would be interested in meeting and, of course, making sure that Nancy was always on the list. She would also point the always fashion conscious Nancy in the direction of wearing outfits created by

McCartney's daughter Stella whenever McCartney was in the picture. But perhaps the most important thing Walters could do was to instruct her how to behave around a musician of McCartney's stature. Walter's strategy was clear: Look at Heather Mills and do exactly the opposite.

The strategy worked to a T. Now both single, McCartney and Nancy appeared relaxed and easy with each other during those dinner get-togethers and quickly progressed to a handful of low-key meetings in 2007. There was only one fly in the ointment.

While the romance with Nancy seemed to be heating up, McCartney was continuing to keep time with Rosanna Arquette. There was a bit of an uproar in the tabloid world when the three-sided romance was made public. But for Nancy, it was not only not a surprise but, apparently, not that big a deal. According to the *London Evening Standard*, Nancy was aware that McCartney was also seeing Arquette and was not overly concerned when McCartney would disappear from her life for several days, preferring quite logically to let it all play out and see what happened. It would ultimately be in Nancy's favor that Arquette, both good and bad, had been involved with several musicians over the years, most notably Peter Gabriel and knew her own need for privacy and being out of the spotlight. How the relationship between McCartney and Arquette ended is not certain but what was known was at some point McCartney was back with Nancy full time and the couple would remain inseparable for the next four years.

Those years would be played out in stark contrast to their previous relationships.

Nancy proved quite adept at keeping things low profile. They were not hiding from the press and would often be captured by the paparazzi on romantic getaways, arm in arm at charity and fashion events and Nancy would often be present somewhere in a packed concert hall, watching her man rock out. But interviews? Nancy would not do them. Getting a no comment from her was considered a scoop. McCartney was considered the family spokesman and that was fine with Nancy. Rumors had always abounded that, once their relationship became serious, Nancy and McCartney sat down and had a long and serious discussion about how they would handle their public and private lives. True or not, there did seem to be a pattern in place that would allow Nancy to happily live in the shadows and continue to have a normal life.

Needless to say, after the chaos surrounding their father's second marriage, Nancy was a breath of fresh air to the McCartney children. They had known her previously while spending time in the Hamptons, often referring to her as Jackie O because of her fashion sense and style. Their relationship would only deepen as Nancy and McCartney became romantic.

She would continue to have her work life with the Shevell Corporation, which occasionally inspired some office gossip, which she laughingly played along with. There was nothing to hide. Nancy was happily in love with Paul McCartney. She continued to have a circle of friends and was fairly unrecognizable when she walked the streets of New York.

May 2011. Nancy and McCartney announced their engagement to be married.

By 2011, Nancy and McCartney were head over heels in love and had been that way for seemingly forever. They had talked about marriage for quite some time and now seemed the time for the next step. Nancy was so in love that it seemed almost unseemly to mention a prenuptial agreement. But Nancy was confident enough in their future to offer to sign one. McCartney rejected the notion and, logically, it all seemed to make sense. McCartney was one of the richest people on the planet while Nancy's wealth at the time of their marriage was estimated at more than $200 million. With the money issue long out of the way, the path to love and marriage was now clear.

Nancy and McCartney were officially married on October 9, 2011 at the Old Marylebone Town Hall registrars' office. There was a sense of joy and nostalgia in the air. The Old Marylebone was where McCartney and first wife Linda were married. And much like other Beatle marriages, hundreds of fans and an equal amount of press were gathered as the couple went swiftly into the building where an hour-long ceremony concluded with the happy couple emerging hand in hand. Nancy was now officially Lady McCartney.

Among the invited guests to an after party was the only other surviving Beatle, Ringo and his wife Barbara. During the after party, McCartney unveiled a new song, "My Valentine," in honor of his wife. By all accounts, Nancy was touched and shed a tear. Then it was off to a four-day honeymoon at the private Caribbean estate of Mick Jagger.

Then it was back to work.

For McCartney it was preparation for an upcoming tour. For Nancy, it would be getting her house in order. For the time being, she would remain in the business world but even that suddenly seemed of less importance. Shortly after the wedding, Nancy would step down from the Metropolitan Transit Authority. And while she still remained Vice President of her family's business, she acknowledged that she would now be spending the lion's share of her time in England.

The next nine years would fly by. Nancy would turn 60 on the occasion of the couple's ninth anniversary. McCartney was now 79. But in their hearts the love continued to grow. McCartney would acknowledge Nancy as only a songwriter could when he offered the world his heartfelt feelings in a Twitter missive. "Congratulations Nancy on our ninth wedding anniversary. Thanks for nine beautiful years of marriage. You are my rock n'roll. You are my A side and my B side. You are my verse and chorus. I love you Paul."

Nancy's response, publicly, was not surprisingly no response. It was not her way. But in her own way, Nancy has been expressing her love and her life the way she always has, by her actions.

As witnessed by UK journalist Piers Morgan, Nancy had the occasion to arrive at London's Heathrow Airport when she was interrogated by an immigration officer who wanted to know why she was traveling alone, who her husband was, where her husband was and what was he up to. This interrogation would go on for sometime until Nancy was allowed to pass. At no point in their conversation did Nancy give her husband's name. After she had gone through, Morgan went up to the officer and told him that the woman was married to Paul McCartney. The officer went beet red and began hyperventilating. Morgan was not surprised by Nancy's actions as he offered in *Quora.com*.

"You don't see Nancy giving television interviews or using Paul to further her career. Nor does she seem to have the slightest interest in basking in the residual glory of his fame. She just loves him for who he is and that's why Paul looks so happy."

Epilogue
And in the End

The Beatles were notorious for lyrical mystery and questioning. The last lines of the song The End off their *Abbey Road* album are a perfect example.

"And in the end the love you take is equal to the love you make."

That little bit of business has kept Beatle completists guessing for quite a while. Is it a cosmic utterance? Is there some kind of philosophical slight of hand going on? Or could it have been an homage to the wives who had been in and out of their lives for better or worse?

There's a sense of yin and yang going on here. Take away the notion that these women were married to somebody famous and you could quite easily equate this to the trials and tribulations of everyman and every-woman. A universal truth if you will, that a lot of salt of the earth 'not famous' people have gone through the same ups and downs. But since we're dealing with celebrity love and loss, let's just assume that the lyrics were about their wives past, present and, maybe, future.

Collectively, the Beatle wives have certainly been worthy of note. They went into their lives with seemingly their eyes wide open, their hopes, fears and concerns visible on their emotional sleeves. They must have known what to expect. Or were they ultimately blindsided by the idea of marriage to a legend? Some were able to handle it better than others and all, by degrees, learned the fine art of surviving as a Beatle wife on the fly.

Reality check. Their husbands were flawed. The wives were often treated shabbily. But to varying degrees they stuck it out. Because they were in love.

One thing was certain. The moment they said their 'I do's, the wives of the Beatle men were forever branded and acknowledged as a Beatle wife, even if, in several cases, the marriages did not survive, forever linked to a past or present spouse no matter their individual accomplishments.

There was no escaping the fact that they were and always would be that historical footnote in the lives of the larger than life men they fell in love with and married. When it was good it was very good and, in the cases where the relationships went south, it would also be a crushing blow that they were forced to deal with.

But it is to these women's credit that, to a person, they were able to go on and either live their lives in bliss or tough it out and become truly independent women on their own. Now you know them. What you think of them is finally up to you.

SOURCES

Introduction

BOOKS
John Lennon: The Life by Phillip Norman, *Wonderful Tonight* by Pattie Boyd, *John, Paul and Me* by Len Garry

WEBSITES
Classicbands.com, Harrisstories.tumbir.com, Beatlesarama.com, Senstarr.com, GroovyPaulie.tembir.com, Contactmusic.com, TodayIfoundout.com

MISCELLANEOUS
Beatle Stories (documentary)

Chapter One—Cynthia

BOOKS
John by Cynthia Lennon, *A Twist of Lennon* by Cynthia Lennon, *Lennon* by Ray Coleman, *The Love You Make* by Steven Gaines and Peter Brown

MAGAZINES
"Uncut Legends," *Living on Mallorca*, "Celebrities in Majorca," *People*

NEWSPAPERS
The Sun, The Sun Times, The Express, The Independent

WEBSITES
ClassicBands.com, HeraldExtra.com, BBC.com, InMyRightMind.com, CynthiaLennonQuotes.com, JohnAndCynthiaLennon.blogspot.com, Merseyworld.com, BBCNews.com, Vulture.com, JulianLennon.com

RADIO
National Public Radio

Chapter Two—Maureen

INTERVIEWS
Michael Seth Starr, author of the book *Ringo: With a Little Help*.

BOOKS
Wonderful Tonight by Pattie Boyd, *The Beatles Here There and Everywhere* by Geoff Emerick and Howard Massey

MAGAZINES
Goldmine, US News, Teen Life, Datebook, Le Chroniquer

NEWSPAPERS
London Evening Standard, The Daily Express, The Daily Mirror, The Telegraph

WEBSITES
WattpadW.com, Beatlesstory.com, Beatleinterviews.org, BornLate. Blogspot.com, LittleWillow.com, TheBeatlesBible.com, TheFabFour blog, Musicaholics.com, WithTheBeatleGirls.com, TheBeatlesUltimate Experience.com, TruthAbouThe BeatleGirls.com, Startsat60.com

Chapter Three—Pattie Boyd

BOOKS
Behind Sad Eyes: The Life of George Harrison by Marc Shapiro, *Wonderful Tonight* by Pattie Boyd, *Ronnie: The Autobiography* by Ron Wood

MAGAZINES
Goldmine, Harper's Bazaar, South Coast Today, Hell.

NEWSPAPERS
Sydney Morning Herald, The Guardian, The Huffington Post, New Zealand Herald, The London Evening Standard, The Telegraph, The Daily Mail, The Times

WEBSITES
Brainyquote.com, ABCNews.com, TheMortonReport.com, TheAge.com, DailyMail.com, Startsat60.com, Mailonline.com, McCartneyTimes.com

Chapter Four—Linda Eastman

BOOKS

Linda McCartney: A Portrait by Danny Fields, *Paul McCartney: Many Years from Now* by Barry Miles, *Yesterday: The Unauthorized Biography of Paul McCartney* by Chet Flippo, *Man on the Run: Paul McCartney in the 70*'s by Tom Doyle, *Fab: An Intimate Life of Paul McCartney* by Howard Sounes

MAGAZINES

Playgirl, Fame, Vanity Fair, Ultimate Classic Roc.

NEWSPAPERS

San Diego Union Tribune, The Daily Mail, USA Weekend

WEBSITES

LindaMcCartney:ABiography.com, BBC.com, Radio Oobu, Joobu.com, LindaMcCartneyWebsite.com, ReadingEagle.com, Brainyquotes.com, TheHitchhikers'GuidetotheGalaxy:EarthEdition.com, Gadflyonline.com, TheMorningCall.com, PaulMcCartneyandLindaMcCartneyABiography. com, LilithMagazine.org,

Chapter Five—Barbara Bach

INTERVIEWS
Michael Stef Starr, author of the book *Ringo: With a Little Help*

BOOKS
Getting Sober by Derrick Taylor, *Still The Greatest* by Andrew Grant Jackson

MAGAZINES
USA Weekend, Playboy, People,Parade

NEWSPAPERS
Queen's Chronicle, New York Daily News, The Sun

WEBSITES
Barbara-Bach.com, TheJohnnyCarsonShow.com, InsideEdition.com, Sentstarr.com,

Chapter Six—Yoko Ono

BOOKS
Lennon by Ray Coleman, *Come Together: John Lennon and His Time* by Jan Weiner, *The Complete Playboy Interviews*

MAGAZINES
US Weekly, Interview, Mojo, Uncut, Humanity Magazine, Ultimate Classic Rock, Esquire, Rolling Stone, Newsweek, Harper's Bazaar

NEWSPAPERS
The Japan Times, Seattle Times, The Art Newspaper, The Telegraph, The Guardian, Tampa Bay Times

WEBSITES
AZQuotes.com, TheDailyMailOnline.com, BriefAndToThePoint.com, BestClassicRockBands.com, InspiringQuotes.com, TheNational.com, GettyRecordingArtists.com, TheGentlewoman.com, TheExpress.com, Pitchfork.com, Madelinex.com, Biography.com, ChrissyIley.com, MomaRetrospective.com, TheSpokesmanReview.com, Access.com

MISCELLANOUS
National Public Radio, Yoko twitter message, CNN, BBC Radio 4, Vicki Sheff interview

Chapter Seven—Olivia Arias

BOOKS
Behind Sad Eyes: The Life of George Harrison by Marc Shapiro

MAGAZINES
Rolling Stone, Record Disc And Mirror, Mojo

NEWSPAPERS
The Daily Telegraph, The Buffalo News, The Sun, The Independent

WEBSITES
More.LAfilmfest.com, PleaseKillMe.com, BBCNews.com

MISCELLANEOUS
Interview with journalist Katie Couric

Chapter Eight—Heather Mills

BOOKS
A Single Step by Heather Mills McCartney

MAGAZINES
Marketing, Vanity Fair, Interview, Event Magazine, US Weekly

NEWSPAPERS
The Guardian, New York Daily News, The London Times, The Daily Telegraph, SF Gate, Press & Journal

WEBSITES
UltimateClassicRock.com, ZeeNews.com, Contactmusic.com, AOL, Interview

TELEVISION
ABC News, BBC. Extra

Chapter Nine—Nancy Shevell

NEWSPAPERS
The Newark News Ledger, The Observer, The London Evening Standard,
The New York Daily News, *The Guardian*

WEBSITES
Popeater.com, Quora.com

About the Author

New York Times bestselling author Marc Shapiro has written more than 60 nonfiction celebrity biographies, more than 24 comic books, numerous short stories and poetry, and three short-form screenplays. He is also a veteran freelance entertainment journalist.

His young adult book, *JK Rowling: The Wizard Behind Harry Potter,* was on *The New York Times* bestseller list for four straight weeks. His fact-based book *Total Titanic* was also on *The Los Angeles Times* bestseller list for four weeks. *Justin Bieber: The Fever* was on the nationwide Canadian bestseller list for several weeks.

Shapiro has written books on such personalities as Shonda Rhimes, George Harrison, Carlos Santana, Annette Funicello, Lorde, Lindsay Johan, E.L. James, Jamie Dornan, Dakota Johnson, Adele and countless others. He also co-authored the autobiography of mixed martial arts fighter Tito Ortiz, *This is Gonna Hurt: The Life of a Mixed Martial Arts Champion.*

He is currently working on the follow up to this book, *Beatle Kids* for Riverdale Avenue Books.

Other Riverdale Avenue Books Titles by Marc Shapiro

Word Up: The Life of Amanda Gorman

Keanu Reeves' Excellent Adventure
An Unofficial Biography

Hard Work: The Greta Van Fleet Story

Lorde: Your Heroine, How This Young Feminist
Broke the Rules and Succeeded

Legally Bieber: Justin Bieber at 18

You're Gonna Make It After All:
The Life, Times and Influence of Mary Tyler Moore

Hey Joe: The Unauthorized Biography of a Rock Classic

Trump This! The Life and Times of Donald Trump,
an Unauthorized Biography

The Secret Life of EL James

The Real Steele:
The Unauthorized Biography of Dakota Johnson

Inside Grey's Anatomy:
The Unauthorized Biography of Jamie Dornan

Annette Funicello: America's Sweetheart

Game: The Resurrection of Tim Tebow

*Lindsay Lohan: Fully Loaded,
From Disney to Disaster*

*We Love Jenni:
An Unauthorized Biography*

*Who Is Katie Holmes?
An Unauthorized Biography*

*Norman Reedus: True Tales of The Waking Dead's Zombie Hunter,
An Unauthorized Biography*

*Welcome to Shondaland:
An Unauthorized Biography of Shonda Rhimes*

Renaissance Man: The Lin Manuel Story

John McCain: View from the Hill